Slingshot

by: Tom Kovach

a collection of the early writings of Tom Kovach

Slingshot
by: Tom Kovach

Copyright 2006 by:
Kovach for Congress (TN-05)
1483 N. Mt. Juliet Rd., Suite 209
Mount Juliet, TN   37122-3315

as a campaign fundraiser
(Mrs. Lynn Kovach, campaign treasurer)

ISBN: 978-0-6151-3770-4

NOTE 1: To obtain an **autographed copy** of this book, please send $25 (includes shipping & handling) to the address above.

NOTE 2: The vast majority of the writings in this collection were originally published online. So, to retain their original appearance, we have left in the underlining where the hyperlinks were inserted. (Any original typos were also left in, for copyright reasons, to retain the original form.) If an electronic version of this book is published in the future, readers will be able to view those links as supporting documentation, as was their original function in the online columns. (Any decision on an e-book will be based on reader input.)

NOTE 3: An audio version of this book will also be considered, based on feedback from readers.

Table of Contents

ABOUT THE AUTHOR 1
AUTHOR'S INTRODUCTION 5
SECTION 1 — MILITARY TOPICS 12
   Did a chastised officer lead to Saddam's capture? 13
   Briefcase Vindicates Bush, Cheney, and West 16
   The Best Revenge 19
   Desert Two 23
   When do I get to meet the president? 27
   Military whistleblower wins another round 36
SECTION 2 — BORDER SECURITY AND ILLEGAL ALIENS 43
   Who will stand up to the Brown Berets? 44
   Will "road rage" become a social barometer? 54
   Tomorrow they ... what?! 60
   "Light up" the borders! 67
   How about "guest" legislators? 75
   Immigration dance: the Texas side-step 82
   President's speech: more immigration dancing 87
SECTION 3 — TERRORISM 92
   Justice for Christmas 93
   Louder than words 96
   The Old is New 100
   Nashville Bombing: Details Sketchy, But Emerging 106
   Nashville Bombing: MND Finds New Evidence at Scene ... 114

SECTION 4 — POLITICS 118
PART A — WESLEY CLARK 119
   The Evil We've Been Spared 120
   Wesley Clark: Discharge Immediately! 123
PART B — HILLARY CLINTON 130
   War as Backdrop 131
   Staple down the tablecloths! 137

STOP Hillary NOW!! *145*

PART 5 — SHORT BURSTS **153**

Short Bursts: Volume 04-01 .... *154*
Short Bursts: Volume 06-03 .... *162*

SECTION 6 — POETRY AND LYRICS **171**

The Ballad of the Liddy Brigade *172*
Standoff *173*
One Day *175*
Why I wrangle *177*

About the Author

Born in 1958, Tom Kovach (rhymes with "watch") is the product of an immigrant family. Tom's grandparents each came from the Carpathian Mountains of Eastern Europe, and met while working in a shoe factory in the Upstate city of Binghamton, New York. Tom's father, František (Frank) "Lefty" Kovach left home at 16, during the Great Depression. Frank started as a carnival strong man, and then became a Golden Gloves boxer. He then joined the Army, and was stationed at Schofield Barracks in Pearl Harbor, Hawaii, from 1935 to 1939. While there, he became the military intramural welterweight boxing champion of the Hawaiian Islands.

Upon returning to the States (at that time, Hawaii was still a US Territory), Frank joined the Merchant Marine. During World War Two, he sailed on freighters and tankers into ports such as Bahrain and Vladivostok. After the war, he worked as a welder in the shipyards of Long Beach, California. There, he met a "Rosie the Riveter" named Hilda, who went by the nickname Jerry. They both drank a bit. (Lefty had made Sergeant — *three times* — in the Army.) On New Year's Eve, 1947, Lefty and Jerry had their last drink at midnight, in a Long Beach bar with their friends. The next day, they married in Tijuana. And, they never drank another drop of alcohol.

During that same post-war period, Lefty resumed boxing. He boxed amateur for a while, and then fought a few professional bouts.

But, the money was never there for him, although his boxing record was fairly impressive (19 wins, one draw, one loss). Frank moved back to New York for a few years with his bride. Then, he got a job driving long-haul trucks. That led, eventually, to a steady job at a chemical refinery in south Texas. Frank first helped to build the plant, and was then hired by plant management to operate the portion that he had built. It paid well, until Frank was severely injured in an explosion that hospitalized him for 18 months while Tom was a baby.

Tom inherited the stubborn willpower of his Carpatho-Russian father, and the vocabulary of his would-be actress mother. She died from medical malpractice when Tom was five years old. Frank died in Tom's arms when Tom was 14 years old. He then moved from his home in south Texas to live with relatives in Binghamton.

His fellow high school students in New York ridiculed Tom for his thick Texas accent, which has since faded as a result. The time in New York filled in many gaps for Tom about his ethnic heritage. (Lefty had never taught Tom to speak the Carpatho-Russian language, nor much about their history. Tom learned those things from his grandmother before she died — two days before her 98th birthday.)

While in high school, Tom joined the Civil Air Patrol as a cadet. In August of 1974, while still a "cadet basic", he became the honor graduate of CAP Ranger School — a non-combat course, patterned after USAF Pararescue training, although much shorter. In only one year Tom earned the Billy Mitchell Award in the cadet program, passed the advanced phases of his Ranger training, and was selected to join the Ranger instructor staff.

In April of 1975, the city of Saigon fell to the Communists, thus marking the final blow of the Vietnam War. In June of 1975, Tom graduated from high school. In August of 1975, Tom went into basic training in the United States Air Force. Tom spent his first three years "mis-matched" as a mainframe computer operator. (He had entered the service with the goal of becoming a Pararescueman. They wear a Maroon Beret, and are known as PJs.) In early 1979, Tom was a distinguished graduate of the USAF Law Enforcement Academy, and then a squad leader at the Camp Bulliss combat school, where he earned his Blue Beret.

Tom's military duties have included both "permanent" (in the military? *ha!*) and temporary assignments that have given him a broad range of skills, experiences, and insights. He has operated heavy equipment, worked various functions regarding aircraft crashes (in both his USAF and his CAP roles), led a USAF Emergency Services Team (counter-terrorism) overseas, done anti-terrorist planning at Stateside bases, served on a protection detail for President Reagan, deployed to Exercise Bold Eagle (which, that year, was the "dress rehearsal" for Operation Urgent Fury — the rescue of American hostages at a medical school on the island of Grenada), worked with Special Agents of several Federal agencies, been a security advisor to various commanders (up to three stars), led and trained a team for a special military competition (Peacekeeper Challenge), and responded to prevent an international incident in connection with high-level negotiations for the release of the American hostages that were held in the embassy in Tehran, Iran. (The details of incident were published in an issue of *Tiger Flight*, the newsletter of the Air Force Security Police Association.) He also invented the Kovach Klip — and got a thank-you letter from General H. Norman Schwarzkopf.

Tom led a team that properly navigated a Special Operations training course in an alligator-infested swamp. He is rated as an open-water scuba diver. Tom studied two college semesters of the Korean language, in-country. While in Korea, he also practiced several styles of martial arts, both on- and off-base. Tom has made 44 parachute jumps, 35 of them freefall. He was severely injured in a high-speed parachute malfunction while in freefall over West Point. Tom is a disabled veteran, but can do most tasks with minimal accommodation.

Tom Kovach is now a candidate for the 5th Congressional District of Tennessee, which includes Nashville and surrounding areas. His opponent is Jim Cooper, the wealthy son of a former governor.

Tom has been married (second time) since June of 2002. His wife, Lynn, is also his campaign treasurer. They each have one child.

Author's Introduction

On one hand, this has been an "easy" book to write — because most of it was already written long before I wrote this introduction. On the other hand, it has been a difficult book to write, because it has taken me so long. But, the journey has been worth it for me, and I hope that reading a little about the journey will be worth it for you.

This is my first published book. But, it is not the first book that I've ever started to write. Before this, I've worked on two novels, and an autobiography. The experience has helped me to grow as a writer.

In the late 1970s, I started to write a novel. It was based loosely upon some people that I had met during the first few years of my Air Force career, when many men came back from war with amazing stories. I'd begun wondering what happens to "old soldiers" (and spies!) when their official careers are finally over. As a young man, I saw that the world was changing rapidly, and didn't like some of those changes. I longed for some strong men to face the bullies, the gangs, and the terrorists that were making society into a bad place to live. (And, I strove to become like the men that I longed for.) At my first "permanent" duty station, I was blessed to meet some of those men, and to read about others. They were the basis for a novel about a group of former Special Operations soldiers, and CIA spies, that would put their combination of brains and brawn together to save America. Of course, they would do it quietly, because some of their deeds were not entirely legal. (Over the years, I've learned that, "What's right is not always legal, and what's legal is not always right.") I made the mistake of bragging about the first three chapters of my novel to a few people. Then, I got orders to Korea. When I came back, I saw the premiere of a TV show that was one of the most popular of the 1980s. And, it was very much like the concept of my novel (which was called *The Drama Guild* — because the men covered their activities under the guise of a dilapidated storefront community theater project.) The TV series was called *The Equalizer*.

In the mid-1980s, I began work on another novel. This one was about a former Special Operations soldier that goes into politics. To give the story a ring of realism, I wanted to insert real-life people into the "historic" portions of the novel — which was to be set about a dozen years into the future. So, I wrote to the White House, and got written permission from then-Vice President George H. W. Bush to use his name in my novel. (In the future setting, he was to become president, and send the military into Ethiopia to rescue besieged American aid workers that were delivering food to the starving people there. Little did I know that it would actually happen, but in Somalia.) The main character of the novel was a USAF Combat Controller that jumps into the country in advance, works with the CIA to set up operations, and then sees the chaos that ensues when our government changes its mind in mid-operation. (Again, little did I know that such a scenario would actually happen, and become known as an incident called "Blackhawk Down".) The chaotic incident inspires him to later get involved in politics, and to eventually run for president.

In the late 1990s, people told me with increasing frequency that I needed to write an autobiography. (That trend had begun in the early 1980s, but the trend increased greatly as the Clinton years dragged on.) I even tried to contact a few publishers, but got the door slammed in my face by the class of gatekeepers known as literary agents. I tried to find out what one needs to become a literary agent, with the goal of becoming my own agent. As it turns out, the only real qualification is that one needs to know the "right people". And, just who are the "right people"? Well, if you don't already know, then no one is about to introduce you. (Now, at last, self-publishing levels the field.)

Demoralized, I put my writing ambitions on the shelf for many years, while trying to earn a living at a variety of jobs. (Some of those jobs proved short-lived, because of residual problems from a high-speed parachute malfunction during my Air Force career.) But, I just couldn't keep the writing bug contained. And, eventually, with the growth of the Internet, I found some outlets for my writing. Having moved from Upstate NY to Nashville in 2001, my first online article was published by WorldNetDaily in 2003. (Because it was a news article, and not an opinion or investigative column, I have not included it here.) The only problem is that there was no pay. But, I loved it, and people told me that I was good at it. So, I kept doing it.

In late 2005, as the remnants of Hurricane Katrina rained down upon my adopted hometown, I began working on an autobiography. And, it is still a work in progress. The title is *Five Smooth Stones*, after the verse that describes what David picked up from the creek as he crossed the valley to fight Goliath. My life has been a lot like the story of David vs. Goliath; so, that's a recurring theme with me. Hence, the title of this book.

In both the case of the ancient sling, and the modern slingshot, delaying the stone's release enhances the energy that hurls the stone. Up to a point, the longer the shooter waits to release the stone, the more energy that it will have when released. I have seen a parallel in life, and I call it "the slingshot effect". I have not heard others use this term, although it may have existed previously without my knowledge. I will give one example of the slingshot effect.

In 1996, I was injured on a job, and then learned that I had been replaced during my recovery from surgery (after being told that they would hold my job for me). I became qualified for a "displaced worker" retraining program. I took a course at a university, and got a certificate as a paralegal. I've worked in a few law offices. And…

That training helped me to fight off the courtroom attacks by my ex-wife and her predatory attorney. (The court branded him a "provocateur". And, it's legal for me to write that here, because the decision was upheld.) Although he had been practicing law for 20 years, and taught a paralegal course at a college (not the one that I attended, thank God), my legal arguments got the attorney sanctioned (fined) — twice! He appealed — twice. He lost — *twice!* To my knowledge, no other *pro se* (a person that represents himself in court) has ever gotten a lawyer sanctioned in New York State even once. And, I successfully argued against his appeals at the Appellate Division (the second-highest court in NY State), before a panel of seven experienced judges — twice. (A couple that I know had the misfortune of having to bring a case before the same Appellate Division. The wife, who is a college professor, told me, "Your papers look just like the ones that we paid $30,000 for.")

There was a spin-off effect from this benefit — although the benefit itself was mighty "fine". While studying at the university, I was introduced to the Internet. By mid-1997, I became self-taught in HTML code writing, and began building Web sites. I've been honing those skills ever since, and built my own campaign Web site.

Having learned how the Internet works, I was able to do online research. I've learned a myriad of things that other people pay some consultant to find out for them. I've learned how "the system" works with regard to fiction writing (my "next big thing", because that is where the big money is). I've written a sample script for television. (It is a two-part script for the now-defunct series *JAG*.) Under the rules of the Writers' Guild of America, I must have an agent present the script to a producer. But, if a producer reads this book, and thus "discovers" my writing talent, then he may approach me directly. So, I hope that several producers will read this book. (And, I plan to send copies to my favorite ones — to help grease the wheels of progress.) All I need is one or two scripts under my belt, and I'll be established as an income-producing writer.

The nice part is that I could write the scripts "on the side", even if I get elected to Congress. (Another resident of Nashville, Fred Thompson, starred in several movies while serving in the US Senate.) Both parts of my two-part script were researched and written in less than a week. And, the second part is 90 minutes. Some people say that such a product is impossible for a first-time scriptwriter. But, much of my life has been spent doing things that other people told me were impossible. At least this one would earn a good income.

None of that would be possible if an 80-pound box of casters hadn't fallen apart as I carried to the parts room, thus injuring me.

That is an example of "the slingshot effect". Being held back by other people (in other circumstances, some of which will be in the autobiography) has made me wary of those people. But, being held back has also enabled me to build up, and to focus, my energies. Being held back by people has helped me to see some people's ulterior motives in a clearer light. I know what to do, and what to avoid.

But, enough philosophy for now. I'll save the *real* philosophy for the autobiography.

Hopefully, that will help you to better understand how those columns, which I've written for free for all these years, have helped to power the slingshot effect in my own life. In turn, I hope that those lessons will help *your* life. And, by your purchase of this book, you will help to pull back the slingshot of my campaign for Congress.

Thank you.

                                         Tom Kovach
                                         Mon, 29 May 2006
                                         (Memorial Day)
                                         Mount Juliet, TN

Mon, 11 Dec 2006

    NOTE: Even the publication of this book has been subject to the "slingshot effect". This book was meant to be a fundraiser for my 2006 campaign for the US House of Representatives. But, another goal of the book has been to learn as much about the publishing process as possible. And, now that the campaign is over, I can reveal to the public that, during the campaign, I had two major surgeries. Those took time and energy away from the book project as well.

    But, true to my description of the slingshot effect, the result has been a much better product. The few people that have seen the pre-release version of this book will see that the changes (although mostly cosmetic) make the difference between a good book and a really good book. My thanks to those that reviewed and commented.

    Although I lost the 2006 campaign, some benefit has come out of the process. One is my selection to join the Executive Committee of the new National Veterans Coalition, and thus to work with retired Brigadier General Charles Jones III. Keep your eye on the news! The NVC is expected to become a powerful political force. The time is right for a Constitution Party president.

Section 1

Military Topics

Given my background, it only made sense to start writing columns with topics that dealt with our military. It is a theme that I return to as needed, regardless of which publication carries my columns. I was the first civilian to write about the story described in "The Best Revenge", after the story was released by the Marine Corps.

NOTE: This was my first online *column* (but, as explained in the Introduction, not my first online article). There had been several news articles and columns, mostly by WorldNetDaily, about the legal case against Lt. Col. West. But, this was the first column to directly suggest that his actions probably led to Saddam Hussein's capture.

Did a chastised officer lead to Saddam's capture?

Dominos blown by West wind

December 17, 2003

published by: MensNewsDaily.com

In recent months, "politically correct" forces — both inside and outside of the American military — were eager to punish Lieutenant Colonel Allen B. West, who had been an infantry battalion commander in the 4th Infantry Division of the US Army. For those that might have been living in a "spider hole", in August of this year LTC West was accused of an assault upon a turncoat Iraqi police officer during an interrogation. The "assault" consisted of scaring information out of Yahya Jhodri Hamoody by firing a pistol near his head. Immediately thereafter, Mr. Hamoody confessed to his complicity in helping to set up guerilla attacks against US Army members, and vomited up copious amounts of information that led to the suppression of future attacks upon our soldiers.

My question is: what else did LTC West's actions lead to?

I believe that it is absolutely no accident that the military and intelligence leaders in the War Against Terrorism suddenly changed their information-gathering strategy in the wake of the successful information-gathering actions by LTC West. For months, those same leaders had concentrated on finding, capturing, and interrogating members of the so-called "deck of cards" — top officials of the Saddam Hussein regime. After discovering how much information can be quickly pulled from a low-level operator, however, it seems that commanders and case officers quickly shifted gears. They went after bodyguards, who are on a political parallel with police officers such as Hamoody. Published reports said that tips about Hussein had increased dramatically in recent weeks — the same recent weeks as the publicity about West shooting near Hamoody's head. It certainly appears that former Hussein sympathizers got the message that West intended.

Shortly after following the lead of LTC West, our Army caught Saddam Hussein.

I believe it is also no accident that the Fourth Infantry Division, the same division that LTC West had belonged to as a battalion commander, was used as the sweeping force to effect the apprehension of Hussein. Partly for operational reasons — because Major General Raymond Odierno's division has the geographic responsibility for that part of Iraq — and partly for public relations, the same commander that could have court-martialed West is now credited with capturing Hussein. Ultimately, it seems that "a cooler head prevailed", and MG Odierno will be proven right by history for not going forward with a court-martial against the man whose singular action may have *really* tipped over the dominos that led to Hussein's capture. (Career military people know that, to survive, you must make your commander look good. West did, but paid dearly.)

The question that remains in my mind is whether, in clearer hindsight, that same commander will exercise his option to set aside his own sentence. And, in the event that MG Odierno is not inclined to set aside the $5,000 fine against LTC West, it can be set aside by a superior commander — such as President Bush. Such a move is authorized by subsection (d) of Article 15 of the Uniform Code of Military Justice, and would send the proper signal to all observers: soldiers, reporters, politicians ... and Iraqis.

Briefcase Vindicates Bush, Cheney, and West

December 20, 2003

published by: MensNewsDaily.com

Six days ago, members of the American military captured the former dictator of Iraq, Saddam Hussein. He was apprehended by Special Operations troops, who were operating with the Fourth Infantry Division (4-ID) of the US Army. Hussein was hiding in his "Spider Palace" — a slightly modified septic tank, located beneath the home of a tribal relative near his hometown of Tikrit.

Late yesterday, senior military officers released the fact that Hussein had a briefcase, described as his personal briefcase, with him at the time of capture. The information found in that briefcase has already led to the arrest of another general of the former Iraqi army. Reports are also starting to surface about the arrests of a number of lower-level guerilla operatives. It is precisely these types of operatives, many of them members of the newly organized Iraqi Police (IP), that have staged many of the attacks upon US and Coalition troops in recent months. Those attacks have accumulated more deaths than the "major combat" that led to the fall of Baghdad. And, it was a member of the IP that was being interrogated by former 4-ID battalion commander LTC Allen B. West. After a loud "close encounter" with a bullet from LTC West's pistol, Officer Hamoody vomited up the names of some accomplices, and the 4-ID went to work rounding them up. Then, as I wrote in a recent article, the CIA and the Army went about questioning more such operatives, and Saddam Hussein was later captured.

Remember all those whiners that were worried that LTC West had somehow violated IP Officer Hamoody's "rights" by firing that pistol during the interrogation? (How can a traitor to his own country, which doesn't even have a government yet, have any rights while being interrogated for guerilla actions against a conquering army?!) Well, it seems that the contents of Saddam Hussein's briefcase may also contain the vindication of LTC West's actions. Our military is busy rounding up and interrogating more IP officers right now. The degree to which they cooperate will be directly proportional to the degree to which the injustice against LTC West is made right. If our government sends a signal that we coddle turncoat guerilla, then don't expect much information. But, if our government gives Allen B. West a medal and an immediate promotion to full colonel, then you can expect a new flock of songbirds in Iraq. So, in the clear hindsight of night-vision goggles inside a septic tank, West was right.

But, wait, there's more.

Remember all those whiners that said we shouldn't fight a war in Iraq? (You can start with the Nay-saying Nine candidates that, until six days ago, had a slight chance of challenging President Bush next November.) Well, that briefcase is full of information that proves that the president was right all along. Saddam Hussein is an evil madman, and he would rather destroy his own country — and those of his neighbors — than give his people any real degree of freedom. Reports have already surfaced that Hussein's henchmen have taken the guerilla war to the next level: kidnapping Iraqi citizens and forcing them to attack American troops. Saddam Hussein is incorrigible. Negotiating with him would be like asking a freakish 45-year-old pedophile to stop seducing little boys with an amusement park. But, I digress. The point is that President Bush was right.

Remember all those whiners that said we shouldn't award money to those big defense contractor companies to provide police organization and training in Iraq? They said that it was merely a ploy for Vice President Cheney to award contract money to his big-oil cronies in exchange for campaign contributions. Admittedly, there is some evidence that palm-greasing may be a factor. Even so, there remains a basic premise that it was the right thing to do. America liberated Iraq by conquering its tyrannical regime. That regime was so repressive that many Iraqis still do not know quite how to behave with their emerging freedom. Thus, some Iraqis would prefer to return to the "devil that you know". Many of that ilk have apparently joined the Iraqi Police. And, if the IP have been infiltrated that much under American supervision, can you imagine how much worse it would have been if we hadn't used those contractors? Cheney was right.

In short, the Bush-Cheney team has been handed the 2004 presidential re-election ... in a briefcase.

The Best Revenge

December 23, 2003

published by: MensNewsDaily.com

On 16 December 2001, while on a dangerous assignment in Kandahar, Afghanistan, a young Marine named Christopher Chandler stepped on a land mine and lost the lower portion of his left leg. He was on a detail with an explosives ordnance disposal (EOD) unit. In civilian lingo, EOD guys are the "bomb squad".

Almost exactly two years later, on the 10th of this month, now-Sergeant Chandler got his revenge — by "living well", as the saying goes.

Chandler's version of living well, however, also happened to make history. You see, Chris got his revenge by becoming the first military member in American history to be awarded Airborne wings while wearing a prosthetic limb.

Jumping out of the C-130 at Fort Benning was the end of a lengthy battle — against his injury, and against the Physical Evaluation Review Board. He was rated by the PERB as fit to return to full duty, "with no limitations". Although that is quite a feat for anyone that has lost a limb — even if one's duty is a sit-down job in a civilian office — it is a daunting task for a Marine. It means that, among other things, Chandler has demonstrated his ability to run at least three miles within strict time limits, and perform other strenuous physical challenges. Airborne School is full of physical challenges.

(Official USMC photo not included in this book, due to technical difficulties in transferring the image.)

The popular television show *JAG* has a character, Lt. Bud Roberts, who also lost a lower leg in a land mine explosion in Afghanistan and returned to active duty. But, Roberts is fictional, he is a lawyer, and the show has mentioned that he has duty restrictions. Chandler is real, he is a Marine, his duty in the Corps is hazardous, and he has no restrictions. The TV show does give a small glimpse, however, into the challenges of a life such as Chandler's. Those challenges are faced with gusto, as described by fellow graduates at Fort Benning. They described his attitude as an inspiration. In a Marine Corps public affairs interview, Chandler explained the examination given to him by the staff before being allowed to enter Airborne training. "They wanted to know if I was even capable of completing the tasks they had for me. I figured I had an advantage. After all, I have one less ankle to break."

Air Force Staff Sgt. Brian Mayer, from US Special Operations Command (SOCOM) at Fort Bragg, NC, said, "He's an inspiration because you have all these perfectly healthy people who wash out and quit while he stays in and makes it. That's a real testament to his character."

"I was in Kandahar with him when he had his accident, and this is the first time I've seen him since then," said Sgt. Ryan Scheucher, platoon sergeant, 2nd Intelligence Battalion, II Marine Expeditionary Force. "If you'd known him before the accident, what he's doing right now would come as no surprise. Both in uniform and out, he's always just been one of those guys who just shuts up and gets the job done. If anything, since his accident I see a little more fire in his eyes."

Many people have been <u>retained on active duty with prosthetics</u> (I met one when I was in the orthopedic ward at Walter Reed). Some people even <u>continue to jump with prosthetics</u>. But, Chandler is the first person to go into the school with an artificial leg and complete the rigorous training. "I think any obstacle in life can be overcome if you believe in yourself," Chandler explained. "I hope this will make it easier for other people with prosthetics who want to go through [jump school] next time. As long as they won't be extra baggage, and they can pull their own weight and accomplish the mission. Hopefully, they won't have to put up with as much as I had to."

This quote from Chandler gave rise to the title of this article. "I don't have to say anything to people who said I couldn't make it. I just graduated." There is a parallel Chinese proverb that says, "The man who says that a task is impossible should get out of the way of the man doing it."

And now, the Marines have one more EOD technician ready to jump in anywhere and dismantle terrorists ... and their bombs. That would be a continuation of Chandler's version of "the best revenge".

Desert Two ...

December 30, 2003

published by: MensNewsDaily.com

By now, most of the civilized world is aware that there was a huge earthquake in Iran, centered near the city of Bam, in Kerman Province. And, by now, many people are aware that humanitarian help is on the way — courtesy of the US Air Force.

As soon as I heard the news that America was providing help, and that the city was located in southern Iran, my mind went instantly back to the disaster that came to be known by the code-name for its location: Desert One. In the early morning hours of 25 April 1980, commandos of the newly-formed Delta Force, airlifted by Marine Corps helicopters[1], were on their way to rescue the American hostages held at the US Embassy in the Iranian capital of Tehran. They landed at a remote location in central Iran, northeast of the city of Yazd. The helicopters landed there to take on fuel from a specially-outfitted C-130 Hercules cargo aircraft which had gone to the rendezvous point by a slightly different route. But, while on the ground, one of the helicopters collided with the C-130, and the area was engulfed in flames. Eight men died, and several others were

---

[1] **Dec 2006:** A slight correction was brought to my attention by Charles Jones III (Brig. Gen., USAF, Ret.). The pilots were Marines, but the helicopters were Navy. He should know. He helped to write the After Action Report for the operation.

injured. At a time when America's military had been "drawn down" (the term used the last time our military had been "downsized"), and we were facing an increasing number of terrorist incidents, the debacle became a huge national embarrassment. That fact does not, however, diminish the heroic efforts of the men involved in a mission that (by the admission of its primary planner, the late Col. Charlie Beckwith) should have had more resources available.

History has a way of sorting things out. Talk-radio programs are already full of discussion about whether we should help Iran. My view is that we should, because it is the right thing to do — the humane thing to do, the Christian thing to do. (One of the things that makes the teaching of Jesus unique is the concept of "going the extra mile" for one's enemies.) I cannot picture Iran sending troops and supplies to help America, if the roles were reversed. At least, not yet. But, one of the reasons that Christianity has survived twenty centuries is because many enemies are converted by such acts of kindness in the face of adversity. A generation from now, Iran will probably be our ally again, and the pivotal factor may well be our help in the wake of this earthquake.

But, certain points stand out that deserve mentioning. Look at a general map of Iran, and note the location of Bam. Now, look at a map that shows the routes taken by the aircraft involved in Operation Eagle Claw (the raid to rescue the hostages). Note that the first place where the helicopter and C-130 routes converge is almost precisely the epicenter of the earthquake. Mere coincidence? Or, did God force Iran to its knees?

The supplies, equipment, and people involved in the earthquake relief operation are being delivered in several aircraft, many of them C-130s. This is the first time that American and Iranian troops have worked together since the hostages were loaded and flown out of Iran during Ronald Reagan's inaugural speech on 20 January 1981. (The Iranians understood Reagan's stated philosophy of "peace through strength".) But, there is another "coincidence" that should not be ignored.

(Official US Air Force photo not included in this book, due to technical difficulties in transferring the image.)

Among the things being delivered to Iran is the Urban Search and Rescue Team from Fairfax County, Virginia. Does that name ring a bell? It should. They were one of the key teams involved in the search and rescue operations at The Pentagon, after a terrorist operation crashed an airliner into America's top military headquarters. The terrorist network al-Qaida, headed by Osama bin-Laden, claimed responsibility for the attack. These facts are now common knowledge. Consider the irony. The same group that pulled people out of the flames of that building will now aid a country that most likely helped to finance the attack upon The Pentagon. God bless that team.

Perhaps, after the relief operations are complete, the government of Iran will offer to provide the United States with a token of appreciation. I have a suggestion: bring us Osama bin-Laden and his personal briefcase.

When do *I* get to meet the president?

August 22, 2005

published by: MensNewsDaily.com

Left-wing anti-war activist Cindy Sheehan is demanding that President Bush meet with her in person. She states that she has that right, because her son was killed in the war in Iraq. Most Americans sympathize with her plight as a grieving mother. But, many —perhaps most — Americans disagree with her using her son's corpse as political sniping bait.

For those unfamiliar with the technique, sniping bait is depicted quite well in the final scenes of the movie "Full Metal Jacket". (That movie was a graphic portrayal of the book Dispatches, by Vietnam War correspondent Michael Herr. I read the book shortly after it was published — long before the movie.) In the heat of battle, a soldier is wounded. He lies on the ground, writhing in pain. His squad looks on from a position of cover. Then, someone is sent out to rescue the wounded soldier. But, just as he approaches the first victim, the rescuer becomes the victim of a sniper. (The technique doesn't hinge upon whether the first victim fell to the sniper's rifle, or was simply injured by any random act on the battlefield.) Now, two soldiers are lying in the open, in obvious pain. (The sniper's preferred targets are knees and ankles, because self-rescue becomes painfully impossible.) It becomes difficult to find volunteers to go out for another rescue, and the pinned-down unit becomes demoralized. Sometimes, the sniper adds to this factor by loudly taunting the unit from a hidden position.

Cindy Sheehan is loudly taunting President Bush, albeit from a very visible position — willingly provided and protected by the "Mainstream" Media (MSM). Any attempts to "rescue" the situation will obviously be met by more sniping. But, because of the visibility and firepower provided by the MSM, the president cannot "disengage and outflank" Sheehan. So, she continued (until recently) to demand a meeting with President Bush.

Pundits on both ends of the political spectrum have pointed out, though, that Mrs. Sheehan has previously met with President Bush. She had her chance, because the meeting was specifically about the loss of her son. She did not have to set it up with anyone, or steer the conversation, or elbow her way past a throng of staffers. She could have said then all the things that she is saying now. So, why didn't she? (In her own words, her direct comments to President Bush were centered on her own emotions, and not on any anti-war sentiments.)

This may sound harsh, but I'll say it. Then, I'll spell out some facts to "put the foundation under it", to paraphrase Henry David Thoreau. Cindy, please move on. (Yes, I'm saying it that way to mock the fact that you've been supported by the Hillary-centric, hard-Leftist, anti-anything-conservative MoveOn.org. That organization is funneling political ammunition to promote Bernie Sanders to the US

28

Senate. The Left-leaning "Mainstream" Media [MSM] refers to Sanders as an "Independent", but he is really an open Socialist.) If she was sincere about being against the war, then Cindy Sheehan had an opportunity to prove it when the MSM was at her disposal after her meeting with President Bush. And, her recent change of tactic — no longer demanding a second meeting with the president — only underscores the fact that she's against more than just the war. My experience in observing Leftist political activities is that they are much more energetic about being "against" things than being "for" things. (That is one reason that I'm a "converted liberal". It was the liberals themselves that converted me.)

There's more logic to my advice that Mrs. Sheehan "move on". Her son was killed in a war. It is an unfortunate fact of the human condition: killing is what happens in wars. But, most of the time, those killings are done "quickly and efficiently". Casey Sheehan volunteered to be part of a quick-reaction team (QRT). The men in his team were killed in an attack by rocket-propelled grenades (RPGs). An RPG round in a vehicle is often instantly deadly to all occupants. The point of these facts is that Casey Sheehan went into the situation knowing the risks, and those risks got the better of him. To read the op-ed accounts, it is almost as though Cindy Sheehan thinks that President Bush personally singled out her son for death. Cindy, please move on.

By contrast, some people die very slowly — drained of life in many ways. In one of the true ironies of this situation, Cindy Sheehan mocked the death of Terri Schiavo as less important than continuing front-page coverage of ... Cindy Sheehan. Terri's family fought valiantly — in several different ways, in at least two different legal systems, over a period of several years — to stop her greedy husband from depriving her of simple food and water in a nursing home. (At their very core, isn't food and water exactly what "nursing" homes are for?) If that isn't an example of "me first" by Cindy Sheehan, then I don't know what is. Those parents — also Catholic, like Sheehan — were forced by circumstance to watch daily as their daughter's health deteriorated, and then our government forced Terri into a days-long "adult-onset abortion". Terri Schiavo suffered death in ways that are parallel to Jesus' crucifixion (knowing ahead of time that it would happen, aching from thirst, having family and friends watch it slowly happen). Cindy Sheehan owes Terri's parents an apology for her selfish article. Cindy, please move on.

In the same article, in her own words, Cindy Sheehan puts Terri Schiavo's case on the same level as news coverage of accused child molester Michael Jackson. But, like the parents of Terri Schiavo, the parents of those children suffered anguish that continued to be prodded for years. By contrast, Army Specialist Casey Sheehan has long stopped suffering. Whether one agrees or disagrees with the war, the hard fact is that her son is no longer subject to the pain of his combat situation. But, sexually-abused children and their families suffer for years after the incident — even if they get help. Cindy, please move on.

OK, now it's time to get personal.

In my own life, I've suffered the loss of a child in a different way. My child was "protected" from me by a drunken Republican judge that had a political axe to grind. In 1994, I was the only anti-abortion candidate in a three-way congressional race. (News reports from "Christian" groups — which claimed that "no pro-life candidate lost a congressional race in 1994" — intentionally overlooked me, because I'm a conservative but not a Republican.) Both the Democrat and the Republican candidates were pro-abortion. Spending only $3,000, my campaign got over 4,400 votes in a 200-mile-wide district. And, my campaign prevented a wealthy Republican (whose views were far to the Left of what most Republicans support) from getting elected. And, after the election, the Republican candidate had a heart attack.

During my 1994 campaign, my first wife left me. (She had been looking for an excuse, and an opportunity to "make it hurt", for several months.) In the wake of the "downsizing" of my military career — for blowing the whistle on an illegal environmental dumping incident — I was unable to get a job with anywhere near the pay and benefit package that I had in the Air Force. Rather than blame macro-economic circumstances, she just blamed me. When the money ran out, so did she. Then, we entered divorce court.

Rather than go into lengthy and painful details, I will simply say that the aftermath of the divorce gave the opportunity for said drunken judge to get revenge on behalf of his Republican colleagues. (In the courtroom, Judge Herbert Ray was unable to read my court papers — first because he did not have the file in the courtroom, and secondly because he held the papers upside-down after sending an aide to get the file. He slurred his words throughout the hearing, and later cited the wrong cases in his written decision. Several area lawyers have told me that they know that he is frequently drunk in the courtroom. But, they refuse to go on record, because they know what will happen to their incomes if they do. The New York State Commission on Judicial Conduct later censured Judge Ray for funneling "law guardian" payments to a political rival — in exchange for him withdrawing from the election for Judge Ray's seat on the Family Court bench. But, that same NYSCJC refused to investigate my five-page, detailed complaint about his intoxication on the bench.) One of my pro-se motions did cause Judge Ray to recuse himself. The very next judge (we've had six!) told me — in chambers, of course, "Mr. Kovach, your combative nature has not served you well." He was specifically referring to my motion — to force an open hearing in my "closed door" Family Court case — when he said that. I won the battle, but lost my daughter.

She has grown up thinking of her father as an abuser. It is not true, and never was. <u>But, truth doesn't matter when facing certain politically-motivated situations</u>. Ten years have been carved out of our father-daughter relationship. The divorce was precipitated by the fact that — in their haste to get rid of this whistleblower — I was discharged without a physical exam (in violation of Federal law, and Air Force regulations), and thus denied even the opportunity for a medical retirement (for spinal injuries suffered in a high-speed parachute malfunction). If the retirement money had been coming in, my first wife probably would not have had an opportunity to make the false allegations against me. (Although things were sometimes rocky, we did love each other, and the financial strain became more than she could bear. Thus, the divorce probably would not have happened if the financial cushion had been there. And, the allegations were only made when she moved to have me thrown out of our home.) Regardless of the money factor's influence on the divorce itself, the money from a military retirement might have enabled me to afford a lawyer to defend against the false allegations of child abuse. (I learned "under fire" to become a pro-se, but at an obvious cost.) It is another unfortunate fact that false allegations of child abuse are extremely common in divorce cases, and that those false allegations reward lying spouses financially. But, that's another story — covered extensively by MensNewsDaily.com.

OK, what's the point, Tom?

The point of all of this personal whining is that one phone call from the President of the United States could change much of my current circumstance, and my daughter's. Back in 1999, when I did some calculations in an attempt to correct the problem within the system, Uncle Sam owed me more than a quarter-million dollars in back pay from my illegal discharge. Our Commander-in-Chief can make one phone call, and order the Pentagon to make my situation right. (All I want are the pay and promotions that were denied me illegally. I'd gladly forego any "punitive damages", in exchange for the money, and the title "Master Sergeant, USAF, retired". They get a bargain, because everyone that knew me said that I was destined to make Chief Master Sergeant … early.)

But, chances are that the phone call will never happen. Why? Simple. I don't "play well with others" when it comes to suppressing the truth. (And, I have information stored in certain places that would be politically devastating to certain people in power. They know what some of it is.) When the president's detractors have relied upon liars for their "facts", I've written about it. On those occasions when President Bush has been right, I've written about it. But, on those occasions when he has been wrong, I've written about that, too. And, it is an unfortunate fact that the Republican Party is no longer the party of true conservatives in America (if it ever was).

During the ten years that my daughter was denied access to her father (her mother would not even allow her to mail me a school photo for most of that time), my daughter became someone much different than the little girl to whom I taught the alphabet. Yes, I know that people change; and, that some of those changes might have happened anyway. But, not all of them would've happened. And, a lot of pain could've been avoided all the way around (even for my ex-wife).

The point is that my daughter has gone through ten years of being drenched in lies, and suffers in ways that she doesn't even realize. Casey Sheehan's suffering was brief. I can do much to relieve my daughter's suffering, if only I had the resources that were wrongfully taken from me. Cindy Sheehan can do nothing to change her son's circumstances — which he voluntarily chose as an adult. My daughter has a chance for a successful future here on Earth, if I could provide certain things to her that I've been blocked from having the opportunity to provide. Cindy Sheehan has no such opportunity, even if the president were to meet with her every day. The MSM reports every little detail of Cindy Sheehan's activity. (Well, at least every detail that is favorable to the Left. There are some things about Cindy Sheehan that the MSM glosses over. I have not heard any MSM report that -- in her own words -- Cindy Sheehan threatened to run over her son with a car to prevent him from returning to Iraq.) And, the MSM does not report that Cindy Sheehan is viewed unfavorably by the majority of Americans — overwhelmingly so when military families are polled.

The MSM has refused to report the aftermath of my whistleblowing, because of the fact that certain Left-wing politicians did nothing about the environmental incident. The MSM purportedly fights injustice, but won't mention the multiple injustices that caused me to lose my military retirement, my home, my first marriage, and much of my relationship with my daughter. (Thank God, despite all the obstacles, we have begun to rebuild it in recent weeks.) The Federal government refuses to obey its own laws and regulations, unless someone in power forces certain departments to follow the rules and to correct their mistakes.

So, when do I get to meet the president?

Military whistleblower wins another round

They just can't get rid of this guy

May 5, 2006

published by: RenewAmerica.us

The wheels of justice grind slowly. But, a recent court decision indicates that the wheels are turning in the right direction for a military whistleblower.

Jesus Figueroa does not fit the stereotypical image of a whistleblower. (That image, though, often defies reality.) He is a major in the NY Air National Guard, and has enjoyed a good — even exemplary — record of service. Major Figueroa is a civil engineering officer at the Gabreski ANG Base, near the city of Westhampton Beach on Long Island. That base is home to the 106th Rescue Wing, which gained fame as the heroes of "The Perfect Storm." The 106th was also the first rescue unit on-scene following the crash of TWA Flight 800, because rescue pilot Major Fritz Meyer saw the mid-air explosion while flying his HH-60 helicopter over the base, and responded immediately.

106th Rescue Team treats an injured pilot in a life raft while another prepares the lift for safety

Major Figueroa's career actually started before he joined the Air Force, and subsequently the Air National Guard. While still in high school, he was a Civil Air Patrol cadet, and a member of an award-winning CAP drill team. In every facet of his military service, Jesus Figueroa has won awards and high ratings. He was promoted to major, and given command of the Civil Engineering Squadron, because of his stellar background.

Approximately three years ago, Major Figueroa was presiding over the selection of a new fire chief for the base. The fire department is part of the Civil Engineering organization in the Air Force. Major Figueroa rejected an applicant with ties to senior officers on the base, and selected someone whose qualifications and loyalty were a better fit for his command. That's when the trouble started.

The base commander, Col. Michael Canders, began to pressure Figueroa to put his crony into the fire chief slot, but Figueroa resisted. He asserted his reasons, and thought that the matter would be put to rest. Instead, there was a sudden downturn in Figueroa's performance ratings. In the budget-conscience world of "downsizings" and military base closings, the low ratings were a serious blow to Figueroa's chances for remaining on active duty until retirement. He decided to fight the system — within the system. Figueroa filed a complaint with the Inspector General's office, alleging that he was being retaliated against — including the intentional delay of his earned promotion to lieutenant colonel — for trying to uphold the integrity of the selection process for fire chief. In the wake of his IG complaint, Figueroa was confronted by Col. Canders, who cited certain information from Figueroa's statements to the IG investigator. Such statements are supposed to be withheld from commanders, precisely to preclude retaliation. Figueroa then complained, within military channels, that the IG's lack of confidentiality had resulted in retaliation by the commander.

Major General Thomas P. Maguire

That decision proved unfruitful, because Col. Canders then recommended Figueroa for discharge. The paperwork went up the chain of command within New York, to the Adjutant General. That is the top military officer in a state. The Adjutant General reports directly to the governor, and is in charge of all Army National Guard, Air National Guard, State Guard, and Naval Militia forces within a state. At the time, the NY Adjutant General was Major General Thomas P. Maguire. (He has since retired.)

Because of perceived deviations from the facts and the resulting injustice, Major Figueroa filed a lawsuit in the state's civilian courts to prevent the discharge. In the court system of NY State, the appropriate court was the Supreme Court. (The name does not correspond to the US Supreme Court, though. In some other states, a comparable level would be called the Superior Court, or the Chancery Court. The highest court in New York State is called the Court of Appeals, which is two levels above the Supreme Court.) Figueroa won an injunction in Supreme Court, and the Air National Guard was prevented from discharging him. General Maguire was named as a defendant, and appealed the injunction.

The appeal went to the Appellate Division, which is in between the Supreme Court and the Court of Appeals. In a recent decision, the Appellate Division dismissed Maguire's motion to vacate the preliminary injunction. Figueroa will remain on active duty, pending a full hearing of the appeal at some future point. Maguire has until approximately mid-June to submit his "perfected" appeal. Figueroa will then have an opportunity to respond to the appeal.

Figueroa serves the ANG in a status called Active Guard and Reserve. Members of the AGR are full-time, active-duty military personnel. They are assigned to a specific job position in a specific unit. Thus, AGR members of the Air National Guard usually remain at their assigned base for the rest of their career. (The Army operates its AGR program differently, and their people tend to be reassigned after a five-year tour.) Members in AGR status are in a unique position, in terms of both payroll status and operational command status. That is because they are Federal troops, but are under State control first. Their paycheck comes from the Federal government, but the overall budget for their unit comes partly from the State. Thus, having attempted to fight within the military system, Figueroa then pursued legal action in State court. Maguire is being defended by attorneys from the NY Office of the Attorney General, while Figueroa's case is being prepared by a private attorney.

Major Jesus Figueroa

Jesus Figueroa has a wife and three children that depend upon his income. He and his family had made plans that rely upon his retirement from the military. Although his engineering background qualifies him for several high-paying civilian jobs, he loves his military career, and he feels a sense of devotion to helping to protect our nation during this time of terrorist threats abroad and at home. He feels frustrated by the fact that a solid track record of duty performance is no longer enough to guarantee continued income and a future retirement. Month after month, Figueroa must keep afloat in a negative climate of office politics, while awaiting the final grind of those wheels of justice.

editor's note — full disclosure

The author was an active-duty member of the NY Air National Guard during the final years of his military career, which began in 1975. During approximately three hours of telephone interviews, the author and Major Figueroa discovered that they had crossed paths at Maxwell AFB, Alabama, in the winter of 1983. While still on active duty, the author blew the whistle on illegal activities by the base commander (then-Colonel Paul A. Weaver, Jr.) at his last base (Stewart ANG Base, Newburgh, NY). Those activities involved the late-evening dumping of contaminated wastewater on Friday, 10 August 1990, using a fire truck to pump the sludge over the fence. (A year after the dumping incident, a news helicopter from WNBC-TV in Manhattan filmed the brown foam that still remained around Silver Stream Reservoir, which is part of the drinking supply for the City of Newburgh.) In the wake of his whistleblowing, the author was discharged in November of 1991, under questionable circumstances. Weaver was replaced by then-Colonel Thomas P. Maguire, the defendant in the Figueroa case. In 1994, the author ran for the 26th Congressional District of NY, which included parts of Stewart ANG Base. Tom Kovach visited friends on the base. Those friends posted Tom's campaign flyers on various bulletin boards. Afterward, Col. Maguire issued a letter, barring Kovach from Stewart ANG Base. But, proper procedures were not followed, and Kovach was never sent a copy of the letter. (He discovered the ban when he tried to visit his friends again, a few weeks later, and was shown the letter inside the gate shack.) Weaver was later promoted to Major General, and became Director of the Air National Guard for the entire country. One of Weaver's last official acts was to hold a press conference, to say that United Airlines Flight 93 was *not* shot down over Pennsylvania on "9-11." Kovach later wrote a five-part series ([posted on RenewAmerica.us](#)) that refutes Weaver's assertion, and shows multiple proofs that the airliner was indeed shot down. After his retirement, General Weaver became a lobbyist within a few months. Federal law requires that senior officers wait two years before becoming a lobbyist.

Section 2

Border Security and Illegal Aliens

NOTE: It's not easy to stand up to the overwhelming power of the "mainstream" media (MSM). A few small groups of people, who share a Left-leaning ideology, control the vast majority of information that we call "news" here in America. Ironically, in the former Soviet Union, the government-owned newspaper was named "Pravda", which means "truth". But, the Soviet citizens saw through the smokescreen, and nicknamed it "new lies for old".

This column is like a research paper to unravel the "spin" and outright falsehoods of the MSM regarding the Minuteman Civil Defense Corps and their border-watch operations. The MSM parroted the allegation of "racism" by a group called the Brown Berets, but did absolutely no background check on the group itself. My research shows that the Brown Berets are a dangerous — and racist — group themselves, unlike the Minutemen that they sought to disparage.

Who will stand up to the Brown Berets?

August 29, 2005

published by: RenewAmerica.us

NOTE: Renew America is the opinion Web site of Dr. Alan Keyes, who ran for president in 2000. He was bumped out of the Republican presidential primary by a combination of vicious lawsuits (by fellow Republicans), and deliberate MSM omission from key stories. In the primary process, I trudged through a New York blizzard to get more petition signatures for Dr. Keyes (to overcome the NY lawsuit). We were initially successful, but the judge eventually decided in favor of the NY party machinery. Alan Keyes was the best-qualified candidate, and the only *true* and *consistent* conservative in the 2000 campaign. He was ignored by the MSM because he is Black and conservative — in other words, a person that does not fit their mold of a candidate.

As I wrote recently, the so-called "Mainstream" Media (MSM) waged a successful propaganda war against what they dubbed "right-wing" militia groups. (That would be groups that organize to protect the United States, and to uphold the Constitution.) Totally left out of that discussion at the time — and since — was any mention of the existence of Left-wing militia groups in America.

Armed members of a Left-wing militia group, North Carolina, 1979 (UPI Photo, from "Red Tide Rising")

A little background is needed, beginning with an understanding of the word "militia" itself. As meant in the context of the Constitution, a "militia" is defined as: the entire body of physically fit civilians eligible by law for military service. Pundits of the Left-leaning MSM have tried to circumvent this definition, but they cannot. The Constitution of the United States makes clear that the Militia is a separate organization from the standing military forces of the United States. In fact, just to clarify that point, President George Washington signed the Militia Law of 1792 — the first law affecting the War Powers of the Office of the President. It took more than one hundred years before a measure would be introduced to Federalize the traditional Militia. Nonetheless, the traditional structure of the Militia still exists on the law books today, because it is still "necessary to the security of a free state".

But, another definition of "militia" is more open, and more controversial: "A private, non-government force, not necessarily directly supported or sanctioned by the government." This definition applies to both Left-wing and true Right-wing militia groups; but, not to the Constitutional militia groups — which the MSM tried to categorize as Right-wing groups. (An example of a Left-wing militia group of this sort would be the "technicals" that stole food from Christian relief workers in Somalia, and brutalized American troops in an incident that came to be known as "Blackhawk Down.") These definitions are key to understanding why the Left-leaning MSM is under-reporting the threat to America by a group calling itself The Brown Berets.

True to its Marxist origins, the group's founder tried to paint the Brown Berets as a non-violent group. In an online Communist-publication interview, the founder of the original Brown Berets claims that the current group is not the same as the one he founded. But, the statements, actions, and motives of the current Brown Berets indicate that they take their inspiration directly from the original, Marxist group in California. And, despite their "non-violent" claims to MSM shills, they also boast that they shot down a police helicopter in Riverside, California, and have killed or injured many policemen.

Carlos Montes, a co-founder of 1967 Brown Berets (Online photo from Communist newsletter "Fight Back")

So, while the MSM portray the current Brown Berets as merely reacting to the presence of alleged "racists" within the Minuteman Project, could there be more to the story? (Isn't finding out the un-reported MSM details the reason that you read MensNewsDaily.com in the first place?) For example, if the Minuteman Project is a racist group, then why did they appoint Al Garza — a former Marine, and a retired private investigator, who lives in Arizona, and is of Mexican descent — as the staff liaison to oversee all Minuteman chapters in Texas? (This was first reported by the Victoria (TX) Advocate, the newspaper of my former hometown, but has been overlooked by subsequent MSM reports.) If there is more, what is it, and does it have an effect upon most other Americans? The answer is "yes" to both.

America is under invasion. This invasion takes several forms; but, the most prevalent — and preventable — is the invasion by land through the porous borders of our Southwestern states. It is also well-known that America is under terrorist threat. And, it is known that Islamist terrorists are taking advantage of the physical similarities between Middle Eastern and Hispanic men to slip through our border with Mexico. And, our so-called ally Mexico refuses to help with border security. These are hard facts, and they constitute a threat to our national security.

"And there's a rose in a fisted glove, and the eagle flies with the dove..."

There was a hidden message in Steven Stills' protest song from the 1960s.

(This emblem belongs to the Democratic Socialists of America. They are the parent organization of the traitorous Progressive Caucus — Communist members of Congress!)

Contrary to MSM myth, Communism is not dead — not even in America. And, the weakening of America is a long-term goal of Communism, because a strong America is one of the last stops between freedom and global domination. One of the ways for Communists to help weaken America is to propagate the phony notion that "undocumented workers" do not harm American interests. (If you still don't think that Communists actively want to hurt America and help our enemies, then read Communist Resolution #666.) Specifically, on the subject of immigration, the Communist Party of the USA resolves that, "Workers are workers, with or without papers. No human being is illegal. We fight for full legal rights for immigrant workers here today and those who come in the future." By odd contrast, the Communist Party celebrates a country that has some of the tightest borders in the world — North Korea. Make no mistake; if the Communists are supporting illegal immigration as a "right," then they also have a specific, anti-American program to import people that will fight against America after their arrival.

As I wrote recently, "Terrorists are Communists, and Communists are terrorists." Both have the goal of weakening the United States, to turn it into a slave-labor camp of their totalitarian dream-state. One group — the Minuteman Project — has stood up, and is trying to help secure the borders of this country. And, now, one group — the Brown Berets — is threatening violence to stop the Minutemen! One must ask, "Why would a group — supposedly comprised of American citizens — want to stop another group of American citizens from securing our borders?" In theory, one would expect the Brown Berets to help the Minutemen, not thwart them.

But, there is a reason why the Brown Berets want to stop the Minutemen. And, that reason is that the Brown Berets — a Communist organization themselves — want to weaken America. The Marxist ideology of the Brown Berets goes all the way back to their beginnings in 1967. They, like many other radical groups, openly side with the likes of Mao Tse-Tung and Ho Chi-Minh. They also openly side with Islamist terrorists. They are part of what talk-radio giant Phil Valentine calls the "hate-America crowd." So, why is the MSM trying to portray the Brown Berets as merely reacting to "racism"? It's an old strategy of the Left — one that goes back to the KGB links to civil-rights "leaders". Much good came out of the civil-rights movement. But, one bad thing was that it gave the MSM the opportunity to anoint Left-leaning "spokesman" for selected racial and ethnic groups. (For example, why doesn't the MSM refer to Dr. Thomas Sowell or Dr. Alan Keyes as "leaders" of the Black community? Simple: they are anti-abortion, anti-Communist conservatives. It doesn't matter to the MSM that Sowell and Keyes have far more intellectual power than Jesse Jackson, Charles Rangel, Al Sharpton, and Kweisi Mfume combined.)

And, the Brown Berets go even a step farther than Communism. Despite their accusations against the Minutemen — willingly echoed by MSM shills — it is the Brown Berets that are the racist organization. The Brown Berets are an affiliate of the "La Raza Unida" political party. It is unfortunate that racial and ethnic tensions necessitated the formation of the La Raza Unida Party (RUP) in South Texas — where Americans of Mexican descent were often the majority, but were under-represented politically. (When I was a teenager, I lived in one of the few counties where the RUP had a candidate on the 1972 ballot.) So, although the La Raza Unida Party was formed with a noble purpose, their organizational energy was later co-opted by the militant, Marxist factions within the Mexican-American community. Those forces — like similar forces within the Black community — try to link ethnic identity with ultra-Leftist politics. Thus, anyone that disagrees with their extremist politics is branded "a traitor to their race" (see: "mi Raza primero"). And, in both cases, racial hatred against Whites is used as a cementing factor. Those three factors (our race is better; your race is bad; cooperating with people of the other race is evil) are the essence of a racist organization. Combine racial hatred with Communist zeal, and you have a dangerous "binary weapon."

RED on top!
(Communism, not racial pride, was behind the "Black Power" movement. Blacks were sandwiched "in between" Communists and the KGB-sponsored environmentalists — as the colors of their flag indicate.)

For the most part, Americans still hate Communism — when they recognize it openly. So, the MSM has helped to conceal Communism from the American public by simply ignoring, glossing-over, or outright distorting the facts about groups with Communist ties. Likewise, the MSM has conveniently ignored the links between Communism and terrorism. (Again, this is nothing new. I wrote before about a declassified British Intelligence report that showed the link between the Nazi Party and the Irish Republican Army during World War Two. Yes, the same Irish Republican Army that President Bill Clinton openly courted during his "peace" negotiations.) What is new is the percentage of the American public that sits idly by and accepts MSM reports as the only truth.

The real truth is that the American government has been infiltrated with Communists at the highest levels. The real truth is that former president Bill Clinton is one of them. The real truth is that Bill

Clinton aided a drug-related crony of the Brown Berets in the "Pardons for Sale" scandal at the end of his scandal-laden presidency. The real truth is that Bill Clinton aided the Brown Berets (and other Left-wing Latino groups) precisely because they are Communists — just as Bill and Hillary work to aid Communism worldwide. (Both the Clintons and the Brown Berets are allied with Communist organizer Max Elbaum — who derides the Clintons for not being far enough to the Left.) In another irony of Leftism, illegal immigration has a parallel with abortion. The government of Mexico wants to keep migration into the United States "safe and legal" — as both abortion and immigration were under Clinton. But, Bill Clinton is no longer in office. So, what will current politicians do to stop Communist militants from disrupting the security of our American borders?

So far, the answer is nothing. In fact, it is less than nothing, because President George W. Bush has denounced the Minutemen for doing precisely what the Constitution says they should be doing. And, in that regard, Bush sides with Mexico, which has denounced California Governor Arnold Schwarzenegger for supporting the Minutemen. By contrast, union locals representing Border Patrol Agents support the Minutemen in their efforts. During the Bush Administration, the United States has allowed Mexico to issue misleading ID cards to illegal immigrants. This is a step away from border security, not toward it. Thus, it appears that President Bush is ignoring one of his highest Constitutional duties: the security of our nation's borders. Back in 2000, I warned my friends that George Bush was not a real conservative. Most of them believe me now.

Regardless of what the Federal government does, the State of Texas has a separate and independent right (and duty!) to secure its borders. Thus, the governor of Texas could call up the Militia to secure the border. (As could the governors of the other Border States.) Instead, the Democratic Party is calling upon the governor of Texas to send the National Guard to arrest the Minutemen. It is a wonder to me that the Democrats still have any members! But, like their Socialist allies, the Democratic Party relies upon misinformation and disinformation to keep their "sheeple" in line.

With both Republicans and Democrats ignoring (or refusing?) their sworn Constitutional duties to defend America from invasion, it seems that voters may have no choice but to invoke "Operation Clean Sweep". Perhaps, then, we will have some elected leaders that will stand up to the "Brown Berets de Aztlán" — before they achieve their stated goal of doing away with America's southern border, and ceding territory back to Mexico.

Will "road rage" become a social barometer?

Which country's rules apply?

January 3, 2006

published by: RenewAmerica.us

If you live in a city of almost any size bigger than Hooterville or Bugtussle, chances are that you've seen an incident of so-called "road rage." Some states have even passed laws about "aggressive driving." The problem with legislation about "road rage" is the same as the problem with "hate crime" laws: it is an attempt by government to regulate thought. There are already laws against improper lane usage, failure to use a turn signal, or unsafe lane changes. In fact, people that fail to follow those existing laws are a major cause of "road rage" for the rest of us! And, that fact may be on the increase.

It would be foolish to attempt to justify the recently incident of deadly "road rage" in Texas. But, do similar incidents across the country have a common factor? And, if they do, then what does that common factor tell us? And, how can that information help to prevent other frustrations, crashes, injuries, and deaths? Furthermore, do programs and laws that purport to "attack road rage" really help to improve traffic safety? (One such program has found a unique way to make money from "road rage"!) If there are laws against thinking in an aggressive way, then shouldn't there be laws against driving in a stupid way? Government has singled out the poor, helpless cell phone — even though "inattentive driving" laws have been on the books for decades. But, they have not passed laws against applying make-up while driving, nor against rich people with lap dogs behind the steering wheel. (Is there a lap dog lobby? There might be one in Tennessee!)

In the recent incident, a van driver was in the far-left (passing) lane on an Interstate highway. A sedan driver was ahead of him in the lane, but not passing anyone. The van driver flashed his lights several times, but the sedan driver did not yield the lane. Then, the van driver passed the sedan on the right. Although passing on the right is illegal in many states — and ill-advised, even if it's legal — the van was blocked from passing properly. But, after passing on the right, the van driver cut back into the passing lane too soon, and collided with the sedan. The sedan swerved across the median, and flipped onto its roof, thus producing the deadly crash. The van driver made several errors; but, did the sedan driver contribute to the cause of the accident?

In 1997, New York began the first specific "aggressive driving" program in the country. (Notably, the program exists, even in the absence of an "aggressive driving" statute.) The New York State Police define an Aggressive Driver as one who: "Operates a motor vehicle in a selfish, bold or pushy manner, without regard for the rights or safety of the other users of the streets and highways." By refusing to move over when the van driver flashed his lights (thus asserting his right to pass), was the sedan driver operating "in a selfish manner ... without regard for the rights and safety" of the van driver? If so, then just who actually caused the accident? (Again, I am not trying to justify the van driver's reaction to the sedan blocking the lane. I'm merely pointing out that his alleged "rage" might not have been the "first domino" in the accident.)

Perhaps you're thinking, "It was only one accident. How does that affect the rest of America?" Perhaps you're thinking, "Hey, wait a minute! The sedan occupants are the 'victims,' and most of them are dead. Don't pick on them." I'm not picking on the dead people. The driver lived, and was not injured. (The people in the back seat died. Were any of them wearing seatbelts? If not, was the driver ticketed?) My question is: did the sedan driver create the "first domino" by refusing to yield the lane to the van driver when he flashed his lights to pass? (If there was enough room for the van to pass on the right, then there was enough room for the sedan to pull over. Apparently, the sedan driver refused, and that is the thrust of my argument.)

Now, that begs two questions. First, why was the sedan in the passing lane if it was not passing? (Section 545.051(b), of the Texas Transportation Code, "Driving on the right side of the roadway," requires drivers to stay to the farthest right-hand lane available, unless passing another vehicle.) Second, why didn't the sedan pull over when the van came up to pass? And, those questions, coupled with the identities of the vehicle occupants, beg another question: was the driver following the rules of the United States, or the rules of another country? All of the sedan occupants were "Indian nationals," according to the local news account. In India, people drive on the left.

Thus, according to the instincts of that driver's upbringing, she was in the slow lane. Was that difference in understanding the real cause of the accident?

If the language barrier, or the "drive on the left" instinct, was the real cause of the accident, then we can expect to see an increase of such accidents across America. Why? Because the forces of political correctness have compelled state drivers' license offices to relax testing standards. Immigrants, whether legal or illegal, may now demand tests in their native language — despite the fact that driver's manuals and road signs are in English. (When I was stationed in Korea, many [but not all] road signs were in both Korean and English. But, foreign aid from America built many of those roads in the first place. And, I learned to read Korean within the first six weeks that I was there.) Because of the unique status of the United States as a beacon of freedom, we attract immigrants from around the world. That's great. But, those immigrants need to learn America's language, and assimilate into America's culture, rather than forcing America to become more like the places from which they escaped. If immigrants refuse to become American while they live here, then one of the social barometers of change might very well be traffic accidents such as these.

Of course, as a pioneer in political correctness, NY State also includes flashing one's lights "[... because they were annoyed ...](#)" as an act of "aggressive driving." (Almost any new car purchased in the past 20 years has a "flash-to-pass" headlight feature. But, who said that law has to include common sense? I'm so glad that I left New York, even though the Upstate scenery is beautiful.) As part of their helpful tips to prevent driver stress, New York actually advises motorists to, "...avoid anger-inducing talk radio ...." Thus, we see direct proof that the State is trying to regulate thought, rather than driving actions. (Doesn't the "victim" of stupid acts have a right to become annoyed? Poking along in the passing lane is stupid, and it causes many accidents. But, stupid drivers pretend that passing in the passing lane is "aggressive.") The Interstate highways were originally designed to be traveled upon at 150 miles per hour by cars with 1950s technology. Cars are now much safer, and more nimble, but the Left wants us to drive at one-third the design speed. I prefer this anti-Nader statement from the 1960s, "Ban low-performance drivers, not high-performance cars!" That is a golden nugget of conservative thought.

Notably, the US Department of Transportation keeps statistics on various factors that cause or exacerbate crashes. Those factors include: speed, seat belt usage, elderly drivers, young drivers, and school-bus accidents. There is no category, however, for accidents caused by people from other countries (legally or otherwise) that don't know the rules, and/or can't read the signs. Similarly, I was not able to get a statistical breakout of immigrant-caused accidents from the Tennessee Department of Safety. This is despite the fact that Tennessee was in the national spotlight for issuing driver's licenses to illegal immigrants. That spotlight was turned on by Nashville talk-radio giant Phil Valentine, whose commentaries on that topic helped to spawn a new advocacy group, and forced a change in the state's procedures.

And, that gets us back to the original concept of this column. If a person cannot read the driver's manual, or the road signs, then that person should not be allowed to drive. Somehow, we in America have become convinced that it's OK to allow more fatal accidents, rather than to "offend" anyone by trying to prevent such accidents. If that trend continues, then "road rage" and immigrant-involved accidents can be expected to increase at parallel rates, thus producing a societal barometer of political correctness.

Tomorrow they ... *what?!*

April 10, 2006

published by: RenewAmerica.us

Activists that support the "rights" of illegal immigrants held rallies in various cities across America this past weekend. Logic is apparently lost on the organizers of those rallies. Rights are for citizens. Illegal immigrants are invaders, not guests, and certainly are not citizens. Therefore, to suggest that illegal immigrants have, or should have, the same rights as regular United States citizens is ludicrous.

big picture, small picture

Some people can't get their mind to grasp the big picture. So, let's shrink it down. Let's see if the same logic applies on the small scale. One night, you're sleeping in your home. You hear a noise, suspect a burglary, and grab your gun. Sure enough, there is a burglar in your home office. He's sitting down at your computer, with your bank card, shopping online with your money. Almost tickled by the novelty and brazenness of the deed, you tell him to sit right there while you call the police. He calmly replies, "I intend to."

As you call the police, things don't go much better. First, the dispatcher asks for all of your personal information — including whether you can prove that you are a citizen — before even listening to any details of the situation. Then, as you describe the confrontation, the dispatcher begins demanding all kinds of information about your gun, and asks whether you are a member of any "racist or vigilante groups." You begin to get frustrated, and ask whether an officer will be dispatched to your house any time tonight.

"Of course not," comes the haughty reply. It's late at night, and your city's police are busy fulfilling their community role by playing basketball with gang members in the housing projects right now. "A police officer would only be dispatched if there had been any actual damage to life or property," the dispatcher calmly explains. You retort, "The damage is ongoing. He's cleaning out my bank account right now." The dispatcher drones, as if reading from a card, that the burglar had no choice, because your affluence forced economic disparity upon the burglar, his family, and all the people of his neighborhood. "Well, can't you at least have an officer just take him back to his own neighborhood?!" "Of course not," the dispatcher replies, sounding startled at the very question. "He's been in your home for how long, now? He has rights. Once he's passed the 20-minute threshold, he automatically becomes a member of your family, according to the Kennedy-Specter Crime Prevention Act of 1994. You should know that. In fact, if you don't get him a cup of hot chocolate and a doughnut right away, I'll send an officer over there to arrest you for child abuse."

parallel universe

If the above example sounds outlandish, think again. Take a look around at the current situation — both in terms of legal theory, and in terms of actual application. People sneak into our country. The invaders park themselves in our communities, and promptly begin to help themselves to things — at our expense — to which they have no right of access. Those things include jobs, which seem to be increasingly scarce for legal applicants. But, those things also include education, welfare benefits, and medical care (have you noticed the growing wait time at emergency rooms over the past few years?).

Frustrated citizens complain, but are branded as heartless or racist. Somehow, we are expected to tolerate the blood-sucking, even when we begin to develop societal symptoms that tell us our own country's health is in imminent danger. This is not only economic health, but also societal and cultural health. America is in danger from the tsunami of illegal immigration. Yet, the Left-leaning "mainstream" media continues to pound us with the notion that recognizing the danger makes us the root of the problem.

the issue is not racial, nor cultural

The Left has used the emotional label "racist" in an attempt to minimize the alarm created when conservatives say that our country is in danger. Let's look at another example. If there were 15 million people lined up along our borders, all at once, with the obvious intent of crossing into the United States, then we would consider it a massive invasion effort. We would demand that the military be deployed immediately. But, because these people trickle in, we are somehow expected to disregard the sheer, overwhelming numbers. Not all of the people that illegally cross into America come from

Mexico, nor do they all do so at the Mexican border. But, the largest single segment of such invaders is, in fact, Mexicans crossing our southern border. We need to enhance our security along all of our borders — to include seaports, coastlines, northern forests, and airports. One of the largest international points of entry is in the middle of America, at the Saint Louis international airport. Therefore, border security does not stop merely by building a wall. But, a wall is a very good start, and two walls (don't forget our northern border) is an even better start.

Legal immigrants, and their descendents, are often the angriest about the illegal immigration issue. Nashville is a very cosmopolitan city, and there are ethnic enclaves from around the world. I have met immigrants — legal ones — that are furious about our porous borders. They paid big money to follow the rules, gain legal access to America, and build up a business. Their businesses, along with those of natural-born citizens, are being threatened by unfair competition from businesses that hire cheap, illegal labor. Convenience store owners from Pakistan, teachers from India, and the American-born Latino owners of Mexican restaurants are all in agreement against illegal immigration. But, legislators such as Senator Ted Kennedy say that, "The American people have spoken," when the illegal people rally for "rights." What about the voices of legal Americans?

People of many cultures have immigrated to the United States, and did so because they wanted to become Americans. That is the difference between other waves of immigration and the current wave.

The current wave wants to make America become like the countries that they left. So, what was the point of leaving?

My own grandparents immigrated in the early part of the 20th Century. Communism was beginning to raise its ugly head across Europe. My grandmother's childhood goal had been to become a nun. But, in 1907, her parents pulled her out of the convent, took her to a port in Poland, and put her on a boat to America at 15 years of age. During the Cold War, people who descended from the Slavic cultures (Poland, Russia, Ukraine, etc.) were sometimes discriminated against, and were accused of being Communists. The reality was quite different. Most people of Slavic descent are the strongest anti-Communists that you will ever meet. In like manner, the modern legal immigrants are some of the strongest opponents of illegal immigration. And, despite the façade shown by the MSM, this is especially true of American citizens of Hispanic descent.

the cruelest cut of all

A radio news sound bite this morning gave rise to the title of this column. An activist in Los Angeles proclaimed, "Today we march, tomorrow we vote!" What?! Can someone explain to me how any American — from any race or culture — can suggest that illegal residents are going to register to vote? Yet, the limp-wristed crowd in Washington has dared to proclaim that, "The American people have spoken."

The activist that made this prediction identified herself as "the only Latina member of the Los Angeles school board," and defiantly proclaimed that "nobody will dismantle bi-lingual education," among other things. (People from many countries and cultures have come to America, and have obtained a fine education. Only people from Hispanic culture have refused to learn the language in order to get it. I don't see bi-lingual education being offered in Korean, or Farsi, or Ukrainian, or Hebrew. Mandatory bi-lingual education fosters intellectual laziness.) Worse yet, though, this activist proclaimed that the immigrant movement would put like-minded people — including *Mechistas* — into public office across the United States. For those that don't know, Mechistas are activists (often gang members) that belong to the Reconquista movement. They believe in the secession of the American Southwest — by violent overthrow, if necessary — and the return of the land to Mexico. (The goal is to re-establish the Mexican border to its locations prior to the Texas Revolution of 1835. That would include all of Texas, New Mexico, and Arizona — plus parts of Colorado, Utah, Nevada, and California.)

There is a name for a public official (even a school board member) that advocates putting people into office that would overthrow the United States and secede the territory to a foreign country. That name is "traitor." The words and actions of that official, and others like her, provide aid and comfort to the enemies of the United States. For that person, and her ilk, to suggest that fellow traitors should be elected to office in this country is tantamount to advocating the overthrow of this great nation. That point alone should be grounds for her immediate removal from the Los Angeles school board.

The US House of Representatives should stand firm on the point of making illegal entrance into the United States a felony. Then, anyone that employs, houses, or supports illegal immigrants would be guilty of aiding and abetting the commission of a felony. That, of course, would include trying to register illegal immigrants to vote, or to put illegal immigrants into public office. If such a law has not been enacted, and if I win the election this November, it will be a legislative priority of mine upon arrival in Washington.

"Today we march, tomorrow we vote?!" I don't think so. Instead, they should be thinking, "If we march today, then tomorrow we'll get deported."

NOTE: Numerous investigative reports surfaced after the pro-illegal marches, showing that Communist groups organized the marches. In my "day job", I work for the Nashville Public Schools, and am a steward for the Support Employees' International Union (SEIU). While trying to get the union's endorsement, I discovered that our union strongly supports the recruitment and importation of, and amnesty for, illegal aliens. I provided copies of the documents to two authors that were working on a book about illegal aliens, and the problems created by compromising on this important issue.

"Light up" the borders!

Overcome the language barrier!

April 18, 2006

---

the background

      The vast majority of my Air Force career (Aug 1975 until Nov 1991, when I was illegally "downsized") involved law enforcement, security, anti-terrorism, and counter-terrorism. Some of those duties were mundane, even boring. But, as the saying goes, our job was "98% boredom, occasionally interrupted by terror." My duties also included recovering "black boxes" from plane crash sites, preventing an international incident (related to the Tehran embassy hostage crisis), designing the security for a high-tech facility, a protection detail for President Reagan, and a "hot offload" or two. I've met people from many different countries and cultures (both in and out of the military), and have conversed with some of them in their own languages. This background gives rise to a suggestion for improving our border security. My suggestion would overcome all potential language barriers. (Even if we printed border-warning signs in every language on Earth, some people can't read their own language.) If elected to Congress this fall, I plan to bring this suggestion to the proper authorities within our government. But, to succeed, the suggestion would need popular support. Hence, this column.

When I was stationed in Korea (1980-81), tensions were quite high. For the first month that I was there, the Tehran embassy crisis was still in progress. Terrorists had attacked American interests and allies. The Soviet Union was occupying Afghanistan. A young soldier from then-Czechoslovakia had attempted to defect by literally running south through the DMZ from North Korea. His bold move was met with machinegun fire — from both directions, because the American and Republic of Korea (ROK — "the South") troops immediately returned the fire that had come from North Korean positions. (How that kid made it through the crossfire is beyond me.) Unfortunately, his bravery was for naught. In an exercise of "diplomatic good will," the young soldier was given back to North Korea after a few days. I cannot imagine what fate awaited him.

Amidst those high tensions, we were stationed in an American compound on a South Korean base. As we patrolled the airfield each evening, the setting sun would illuminate a bare spot in the forest that overlooked the base from a steep mountainside. The spot was bare because all the trees had been burned away during an incident a few years prior. From that spot, a team of North Korean commandos had been spying on our base from the mountainside. The presence of the commandos became known after hikers came upon the campsite of a family that had been hacked to pieces. The brutal murders were the result of the fact that the family of campers had stumbled upon the commandos. The hikers reported their findings to ROK authorities. They sent out the ROK Rangers to hunt for the spies. When the ROK Rangers caught the North Korean commandos, they tortured information out of them, then hacked them to pieces, then set the entire area on fire. Hence, the blank spot on the mountain overlooking our base.

(If you ever see a soldier wearing an emblem on his chest — showing a knife encircled by a chain — do not pick a fight with that man! ROK Ranger training is brutal. I was on a volunteer waiting list for that school, but did not attend it. Later, when I was at a drop zone with some members of ROK Special Forces, they described the training. It was one of the few times that I was ever glad that I did not take up a challenge.)

Because of the high level of tensions, the ROK Army had an effective method for helping to ensure the security of our base. They did not employ this method very often. But, they didn't need to, because word of the technique was enough to deter intruders.

I propose that we use the same technique on our American borders.

the technique

At random intervals, in random locations around the perimeter of the base, the ROK Army would suddenly "light up" the area. Most times, they would use spotlights and/or illumination flares. But, if needed, they would "light up" the area with weapon fire.

One thing that our American military possesses is overwhelming, accurate firepower. We have the ability to "place metal on target" anytime, anywhere, in any weather, day or night. For the privileged few that have heard the "dragon burp" of an AC-130 Spectre gunship, and lived to tell about it, the sound is able to overcome any and all language barriers immediately. And, the sight of the destructive power of one of those night-fighting birds is enough to deter even the greediest "coyote" along the border. (News video from Afghanistan showed a car, which had previously contained terrorist leaders, after a Spectre visit. All it contained in the video was holes — hundreds of them.) From three miles up in the sky, on a cloudy night, the Specter can discern friend from foe on the ground with precision. It can put a 7.62mm bullet into every square foot of a football field in two seconds. (Check out this photo, called "Afghani Tornado".) It can put a howitzer round down on top of a tank before the tank can detect the airplane's presence. This is in addition to the firepower of troop-carried or vehicle-mounted weapons on the ground, helicopter gunships, or the new unmanned aerial vehicles (UAVs) — some of which carry weapons in addition to sensors.

So, let's start "lighting up" America's borders.

AC-130 "Spectre" gunship in level flight (official USAF image)
(NOTE 1: Fore to aft: Sensor pods, 20mm Gatling, 40mm Bofors, 105mm Howitzer)
(NOTE 2: Some older models have dual 7.62mm Gatling guns, instead of the 20mm)
(NOTE 3: Also see "Ghostriders in the Sky", and "Spooky" for in-action photos.)
(NOTE 4: Turn your speakers on, and watch this video of a Spectre in action.)

The Constitution of the United States requires that the Federal government, via its military forces, secure the borders of our nation. (Preventing invasion is a military duty, not a law enforcement task.) My suggestion is that we station our military forces — Active, Guard, and Reserve; plus, the activated Militias of the several states (yes, that means that states would start paying the Minutemen that currently volunteer) — along the entire length of both of our main borders. Then, at random intervals, in random locations, our troops would begin to "light up" the border regions. (To be fair, we could send Civil Affairs or Military Police troops to homes in the affected areas, in advance, to let resident citizens know that things will be a bit noisy that night.)

And, of course, the selection of locations for these activities would not be entirely random. By various sources, we can gather intelligence about the planned activities of illegal invaders — drug traffickers, terrorists, human smugglers, foreign troops, and job-stealers — that might attempt to cross our borders in any particular location. When intelligence and surveillance indicates that such invaders are within two miles of our borders, the guns would start blazing. Given the type of terrain, and the sparse population, the sound would carry far enough to deter most people. And, the ones that continue toward the border would do so with the sure knowledge that they are about to have a confrontation with a determined military force.

the precaution

A couple of years ago, I had the privilege of interviewing — first by e-mail, and later by phone — US Army Lieutenant Colonel Allen B. West. He was the infantry battalion commander that scared information out of a turncoat Iraqi police officer, Yahya Jhodri Hamoody. The information led to the acquisition of significant intelligence information. That information thwarted insurgent attacks, thus saving American and Iraqi lives. Further, the network of terrorists and traitors that was uncovered by that acquisition led to the capture of Saddam Hussein. The "first domino" in this successful chain of events occurred when LTC West fired a pistol near the head of Mr. Hamoody. Seconds later, the intrepid commander and his staff were writing down information as fast as it could spew out of the traitor's mouth.

What does the incident with LTC West have to do with border security? Plenty! You see, LTC West did not shoot Mr. Hamoody. He simply fired a pistol very close to his head. There was, of course, an implication that if Mr. Hamoody did not begin to provide needed information, the next bullet would go through his ears instead of near them. And, the technique worked — without any permanent damage to Mr. Hamoody.

In like manner, I am not proposing that we go around randomly shooting people that are contemplating an illegal penetration of our national borders. Of course, if the sights and sounds of all those weapons don't deter the planned penetration, then at least the people will know exactly what they're up against. And, because such demonstrations of firepower transcend all language barriers (and are visual enough to be fully understood by Deaf border-crossers), then there can be no cry of "foul" if a confrontation becomes necessary. And, since many border penetrations are done in groups, there will be a ready supply of manpower to carry any bodies back to the side of the border where they started. To make sure that our intentions are clearly understood, with no chance for random casualties, our government could build any future walls a half-mile inside the border. Everything between the wall and the border could be a free-fire zone. I'm confident that, if such a plan is implemented, news of it will spread to even the remotest jungle village in Guatemala within two weeks. And, when that word gets out, there will — hopefully — no longer be a need to actually pull the trigger.

the wimp factor

There are actually some people within America that will attempt to say that such a concept is "unfair," or that it is "too harsh". As was reported by the Center for Immigration Studies, Mexico is harsh with those that enter Mexico illegally. And, even some within the Mexican government admit blame for the hordes that enter the United States from that country. Despite these facts, and despite the fact that non-citizens have no "right" to demand a free ride in America, Senator Ted Kennedy and other Leftists kowtowed to illegal immigrants by saying, "The American people have spoken." Actually, Senator Kennedy, the American people will speak on Election Day. Hopefully, they will say, "You're fired!" (I'm hoping that the voters of middle Tennessee will say the same thing to my opponent, Jim Cooper, who voted against the Border Protection, Antiterrorism, and Illegal Immigration Control Act.) And, if necessary, the American people will speak along the borders. If they do, they might just say, "Open fire!"

How about "guest" *legislators?*

Can they take what they dish out?

April 23, 2006

published by: RenewAmerica.us

This past Wednesday (19 Apr, Patriot's Day in many states), I spoke at a rally against illegal immigration. The rally was part of a nationwide petition drive, sponsored by the Minuteman Civil Defense Corps. A key member of that group, Tony Dolz, is driving across America — from Santa Monica, CA, to Washington, DC — to deliver petitions to Congress. The petitions tell our Federal legislators to stand firm against illegal immigration, and against any form of "guest" worker program or amnesty.

Tony Dolz is a remarkable man. He is of German descent, but his ancestors moved to Cuba. He grew up speaking Spanish. His parents came to America — legally — when he was young. He was later naturalized, and is a proud United States citizen. He is so proud of his status that, last year, he set aside his several business interests, and volunteered to serve with the Minutemen on our southern border. Now, in addition to conducting a one-man nationwide drive ("A Minuteman Goes to Washington"), he is running for a State Assembly seat in California. And, although the district has a history of Left-leaning votes, recent polls suggest that the immigration issue could carry Dolz to victory.

America needs more citizen-statesmen at every level of government. What's the difference between a politician and a statesman? Here are two answers. First, it's the same as the difference between a salesman and a consultant. (A salesman tells you "what you want to hear"; a consultant tells you the facts, and guides you toward an informed decision.) I don't know if John Trochman coined this saying, but I first heard it while watching video of his testimony at a Congressional hearing. **"A politician works for the next election. A statesman works for the next generation."** The people running the Minuteman Civil Defense Corps are definitely statesmen.

it's in the details...

In the aftermath of the high-speed parachute malfunction that I experienced during my military career, I spent six weeks at Walter Reed Army Medical Center. (I was sent to an Army hospital, rather than an Air Force hospital, because they have more experience with that type of injury. I had been folded in half backwards.) As part of my rehabilitation, to encourage walking, I was allowed to take day trips in the DC area. One of my trips was to the Capitol of our nation.

I'm a detail guy. One of the details that stand out in my memory is a little sign in the hallway leading to the entrance of the Senate gallery. The gallery is where visitors sit and watch the actual Senate proceedings on the floor below. There is a velvet rope, on stanchions down the middle of the hallway. On top of the first stanchion is a sign that says, "Keep Left." At the time that I visited, the Democrats controlled both houses of Congress. (I've often wondered if, after 1994, that sign was changed to "Keep Right." Given what I've seen, on a variety of issues, I really doubt it.)

Little things mean a lot. In America, our custom is to walk on the right. We drive on the right. Our driving rules came from our walking customs. So, I thought it quite arrogant of the Congress to force Americans to violate our own traditional customs, in the very place where those customs should be most protected and preserved.

The above thought might help to explain what's wrong in the current political debates over illegal immigration. The Congress seems to think that American traditions, and the obvious will of the American people, are immaterial. Instead, they seem to think that they are the repository of some special knowledge, which mere mortals out there in Heartland America cannot access. (That is the same thought process as something known as the "Gnostic heresy" in Christian apologetics. It is the essence of elitism — which fuels such movements as the Communist "dictatorship of the proletariat.") It is because of this elitist mentality that Congress is still considering "guest worker" status for those millions of foreigners that have invaded our borders.

parallel universe

Regular readers know that I often like to present a "parallel universe" to explain ideas that go against the so-called "mainstream." I'd like to present a parallel universe that — hopefully — will scare many of our politicians into becoming statesmen. (And, if that doesn't work, will motivate many voters into "throwing the bums out" and electing real statesmen in place of the current politicians.)

Consider the concept of "guest" legislators!

What is a "guest legislator"? Simple. It is a person that has not been elected, has not participated in any type of training, and has no legal claim on a seat in a legislative body. This "guest legislator" might also be known as an "undocumented legislator," because they will have no pass to get into the building. (Of course, if any police officer tries to prevent them from entering, all the "guest legislator" needs to say is, "Don't you know who I am?") Current legislators have nothing to fear from the presence of "guest legislators," because they are only there to "do things that politicians won't do."

How does one become a "guest legislator"? Simple. First, you and all your friends make phone calls to the offices of current politicians. (Please do not try this on real statesmen, such as Congressmen Tom Tancredo or Ron Paul.) Call the politicians all sorts of names for their elitist policy of having police officers guard the doors of the Capitol. Tell them that your ancestors used to live in mud huts on that very ground; therefore, it is your right to have an office there. Then, when they laugh at you, have all your friends go to one door of the building, hold a noisy rally, and make threatening remarks. Then, while all the police go to that door, you sneak in through a door at the other end of the building. Poof! You are now a "guest legislator."

What does one actually "do" during one's tenure as a "guest legislator"? Well, first, go and take a seat in some politician's office. Then, call the office of the Clerk of the House. (Or, the Clerk of the Senate, if you happened to "go north" in your migration.) The current salary for all Senators and Representatives is $165,200. So, call the Clerks and tell them that you will work for half of that — especially if they will pay you under the table. (Even if they pay you over the table, it would equal picking lettuce for $50/hour for ten months of the year.) When a current politician finds out what you're doing, and tries to complain that you are "depressing the wages" in his job market, have all your friends hold a rally in front of a liberal TV station, and have them say that you pay your fair share of taxes (even though everyone knows it isn't true), and that Congressman So-and-So is a "racist" — even if you are of the same race. If that doesn't work, then invent some word, such as "guestophobe." Besides, the only reason that you're there, fulfilling a valuable role, is to do things that politicians won't do.

How long can one remain a "guest legislator"? Well.... What is the definition of the word "temporary"? (The last guy in the White House needed an entire team of lawyers to develop a four-paragraph definition of "is" — and another team of lawyers to develop a four-paragraph definition of "sex.") Whenever anyone tries to tell you that you have no right to be there, or to do what you're doing, tell them that, "No human being should be illegal." If Congressman So-and-So tries to argue that you just quoted the Communist Party, don't worry about it. Your buddies in the MSM will make him look like a buffoon for daring to try to tell the public the truth. After all, your presence there should be celebrated — not merely tolerated — because you're only there to do things that politicians won't do.

Now, if the politicians do manage to get up enough resolve to call the police, and if the police are not too busy rounding up dozens of other "guest legislators" in other parts of the Capitol complex, and if they do manage to toss you out of the building, don't worry about it. Why? Because you'll be able to get back in soon enough. After all, your presence in the Capitol is needed — to do things that politicians won't do.

If any politicians are reading this, and if you don't like my scathing mockery of your limp-wristed refusals to act in accordance with our Constitution, then all you have to do is: 1) become a statesman, 2) secure our borders immediately, and 3) deport the illegals. If you can't take it, then don't dish it out. We real Americans are tired of having our jobs stolen. We're tired of having our taxes raised to educate the children of people that shouldn't be here. We're tired of waiting in long lines at the emergency room. It's time for politicians to become unemployed, so that statesmen can have job opportunities.

See you after Election Day.

NOTE: After the publication of this column, I got the campaign endorsement of the **Team America PAC**. That is the PAC that was founded by Congressman Tom Tancredo to combat this invasion by illegal aliens. It felt like earning the Green Beret of politics! I put out a news release; but, as usual, the MSM did not publish it. That's why I need to publish a book like this, so that patriotic citizens can learn about "the news that the media just won't report".

Immigration dance: the Texas side-step

No border = no country

May 13, 2006

published by: RenewAmerica.us

I grew up in south Texas, before moving to Upstate NY as a teenager. I learned to dance the "Cotton-Eyed Joe" long before I learned that it had ethnic roots in the mountains of Eastern Europe. (That's where my grandparents came from — as legal immigrants.) And, one doesn't need to grow up in Texas to learn how to dance the "Texas two-step." But, this coming Monday (15 May 2006), y'all better get ready for a new political dance: the "Texas side-step."

(How I wish that I could take credit for that concept. But, for those that aren't old enough to remember, it comes from the Broadway musical, and later movie, "The Best Little Whorehouse in Texas." Charles Durning's version of the side-step was absolutely side-splitting.)

My campaign for Congress is based upon many conservative principles. I have never been a single-issue voter, and am not a single-issue candidate. But, there is one issue that has voters totally focused right now. To condense the argument down to a sound bite that might actually make it into the broadcast news, I've learned to simply say, **"No border equals no country."**

Illegal immigration is the number-one hot-button issue in American politics today. News reports that our own government has leaked the locations of Minuteman volunteers to the Mexican government has made the situation far worse for President Bush than he seems to realize. Now, he plans to address the nation with his "plans" to deal with this issue. Get ready for the Texas side-step! And, this time, there's nothing funny about it.

In an apparent trial balloon, the Bush administration has recently "leaked" the idea that perhaps the president would consider putting the military along our borders. Oddly, both the news media and even members of Congress have echoed the mantra that it is "currently illegal" to put the military along the borders. Thus, these "experts" claim, new legislation would be necessary to "allow" troops to be stationed along the borders. Hello?! Doesn't anyone read the Constitution anymore?

[Article I, Section 8, Paragraph 14](#) of the Constitution empowers the Congress for "calling forth the Militia to execute the laws of the Union, suppress insurrections, and repel invasions." Only an idiot can convert that into "currently illegal" to put troops along our borders! And, the term "idiot" would also apply to anyone that doesn't view 15 to 20 million people sneaking into our country as an "invasion." Minuteman co-founder Jim Gilchrist refers to it as a "stealth invasion."

As I've written before, if invoked in its purest sense, "calling forth the Militia" would mean that our Congress would actually provide money to the states to pay the Minutemen that currently volunteer "to do the jobs that our government won't do." Although the purest sense would also be the best sense, I'll settle for active duty troops from our Regular branches of the Armed Forces, supplemented by Guard and Reserve forces, stationed full-time along the entire length of our borders. And, let's put some troops at all of our ports of entry, including international airports, while we're at it.

Would such a program be expensive? Yes. Would it be cheaper than another "9-11"? Definitely. And, if we can afford to secure the border between South Korea and North Korea, then why can't we seem to afford to secure our own borders? If we can afford to send troops into the Balkans to defend the Muslims in a religious war (so that they can attack us), then why can't we seem to afford to secure our own borders? If we can afford to send troops into Haiti, to install and support a Leftist madman, then why can't we seem to afford to secure our own borders? If we can send our Special Operations Forces to train with those of Communist China (a nation that wants to destroy America), then why can't we seem to afford to secure our own borders? If we can send our troops for recurring training exercises with the Egyptian military, which then bombs and burns ancient churches, then why can't we seem to afford to secure our own borders? So, if anyone says that we don't have enough troops to do the job, then I can quickly suggest some locations where we can find some. (Of the above, the only location where keeping our troops might be justified is the Korean Peninsula. The DMZ between the North and the South is the most heavily guarded border in the world.

Doesn't it make sense to train our troops for foreign border service by first guarding our own borders?)

I try to take my task of writing very seriously. And, I'm regularly disappointed with the coarseness of discussions in modern America. Thus, I know that we (and I) should avoid using naughty words. In several years of published columns, I think that I've only done it once before. But, if any elected official — especially the President of the United States — comes before the public to tell us that it is "illegal" to station troops on our borders, or that waves of invaders are our "guests," then there is only one proper reply left. "Don't piss on my shoes and then tell me it's raining!"

Our military is half the size that it was at the end of Desert Storm in 1991. At the start of Desert Storm, it was half the size that it was at the end of the Vietnam War in 1975. And, at that time, it was half the size that it was in 1961, when our own US State Department published a little pamphlet called "Freedom From War." That pamphlet contained the concept of a plan, which has been followed by both Democrats and Republicans, to shrink our American military, while expanding the power and "authority" of the United Nations. Too many of our citizens have sat idly by and let it happen. But, now that our very security — perhaps even our existence as a nation — is being threatened, perhaps more people will wake up. Globalism is a real threat to American sovereignty and security. And, many of our elected officials are globalists. The issue of border security is a watershed issue. Any elected official that will not strongly support border security, and put the "boots on the ground" to enforce it, is someone that has sold out America to a globalist agenda. The agenda has been around a long time. But, it has never been so close to success as it is right now. What will we do about it?

If the answer is "nothing," then enjoy watching, and dancing, the side-step ... all the way to the sheep pen. And, if you don't have a dance partner, then there are tens of millions of illegal aliens that will be happy to escort you.

President's speech: more immigration dancing

"Electronic slide" instead of "Texas side-step"

May 16, 2006

published by: RenewAmerica.us

In a column this past weekend, I predicted that President Bush would dance the "Texas side-step" in his recent speech about illegal aliens. On the optimistic side, he didn't do that. On the down side, he instead danced the "electronic slide."

The speech reminded me of the old saying that "half a loaf is better than none." But, when the speaker is the sitting President of the United States, and the topic is the security of our national borders, half a loaf is simply not acceptable. As I've said and written many times in recent months, "No border equals no country."

Trying to be optimistic, I will credit the president for finally giving in to public pressure to put military troops on the border. But, even that measure is "too little, too late, and too bad." President Bush proposes sending "as many as" 6,000 National Guard troops to the border. He should have said "as few as," because that number is woefully inadequate. And, he immediately disclaimed the program by emphasizing that the troops would be in a "support" role, "assisting" the Border Patrol, and that the troops would not have any enforcement duty or authority. Oh, really?

Border security is the number one priority of the government. If we cannot secure our borders, then we lack both a consistent national identity and international respect. Let's shrink that concept down. If a boy goes to school every day, and drops his books all along the sidewalk, and then keeps walking as though nothing had happened, then that boy lacks a consistent identity as a student. It becomes obvious that he doesn't care. He loses self-respect, and regards himself as a loser. Soon, so do the people around him. They begin to regard him as a fool. Then, the bullies will begin to swarm around him. If he comes to school, but doesn't care about his books, then perhaps he doesn't care about his lunch money, either. It won't take the bullies long to find out. The poor student has failed to secure his borders, and then he suffers invasion.

the "electronic slide"

President Bush proclaimed that a large part of his border security "plan" is to deploy the latest electronic surveillance measures along the border. He "hopes" to have a working high-tech program in place by 2008. But, illegal aliens plan to cross our borders today, tonight, tomorrow, tomorrow night, et cetera. We don't have time to wait for Predator aircraft over our borders. We need boots and rifles along our borders — now!

Trojan horse

But, wait, there's more! There are a couple of old sayings that apply here. One is: "When nothing is happening, something is happening!" Another is: "Beware of Greeks bearing gifts." For those voters that graduated from a public school any time in the past decade, a history lesson is probably needed at this point. The ancient Greeks attempted to siege the city of Troy, but they failed. Ostensibly, they offered a gift in tribute to the superior Trojans. But, the giant wooden horse was hollow inside. Greek soldiers hid inside the statue, which was wheeled up to the gates of Troy. After the Trojans accepted the gift, the Greek soldiers snuck out at night, let in their compatriots, and destroyed Troy. The proposal to issue "smart ID cards" to foreign workers is a Trojan horse, which will eventually ensnare American citizens. (By the way, recent public school graduates, the words "ostensibly," "compatriots," and "ensnare" may be found in a good dictionary.)

William Casey, who was Director of Central Intelligence under President Ronald Reagan, had a memorable quote during the Iran-Contra affair. Casey said, as quoted in Oliver North's book *Under Fire*, "The best covert operation is one that you get your enemies to pay for." If someone has a globalist agenda, what better way to implement it than to get sovereign American citizens to back a program that will eventually be their own undoing? President Bush proposed requiring smart ID cards to every foreign worker. Once the program is funded by Congress, then R&D money becomes available to "the usual suspects" — the companies that hire "graybeard" lobbyists to gain lucrative, high-tech defense contracts. Once those companies have developed the cards for foreigners, it will be that much easier for our own government to require Americans to carry such cards. Thus, our country begins the "electronic slide" toward totalitarianism.

There is another step in this "electronic slide." The surveillance technology that can be implemented along our borders can also be deployed inside our borders. In like manner as the ID cards, money used to develop a "limited" program makes possible an expanded program later. We already have radar-triggered cameras that issue traffic tickets automatically. We already have a variety of surveillance cameras in cities across America. But, if we focus on technology along our borders, it will become easier to deploy that same technology in our cities. Just as C. Everett Koop and Frank Schaffer warned against the "slippery slope," I'm warning against the "electronic slide."

In a recent news interview, I told a reporter that the cost of a single unmanned aerial vehicle (UAV, such as a Predator) could instead pay for a lot of wall or fence. President Bush is focusing too much on technology, and seems intent on ignoring basic physical security. Perhaps it's true that a Predator can find a lot of people, but a wall can stop a lot of people. We don't need to round up more people to clog our courts. We need to deter more people from entering the border in the first place. Taking several years to put costly, high-tech devices along our borders is not an acceptable security plan. Building a wall, and stationing troops along that wall, is a security plan that will simply work.

Whether by means of the "Texas side-step" or the "electronic slide," President Bush is dancing around his Constitutional duty to secure the borders of the United States. This almost seems designed to hand the Democrats victory in the 2006 congressional elections, and perhaps even the 2008 presidential election. Voters should closely check out this year's slate of candidates, and reject any that have danced around the problem of the illegal alien invasion.

NOTE: In covering the story of President Bush's speech, the local *Tennessean* daily newspaper came to the home of an activist on this issue. I had also been invited to her home, precisely to be a member of the group to be interviewed.

This point is significant because the *Tennessean* had not covered my initial news release in January, nor come to my kickoff press conference in February, nor covered any of my news releases for several months. The first coverage of my campaign came only because someone else invited me to their home.

But, there's no media bias…

Section 3

Terrorism

NOTE: My duties in the Air Force included anti-terrorist planning at Stateside bases, and leading a counter-terrorist team overseas. I began paying attention to the topic when I was in high school, and have continued to read about it for the past thirty-plus years. My columns take advantage of the long-term view, and my access to information that had been classified at the time that I first read it. The MSM has a habit of glossing over certain "inconvenient truths", especially on the topic of terrorists and their motivations: terrorists are Leftists!

NOTE: This column contains information that I had refrained from writing about for almost twenty years. But, that information needs to get out to the American public, so that they can understand that not all of our leaders — not even all of our *military* leaders — have the best interests of our country and our troops in mind.

Justice for Christmas

Apparently unrepentant

December 26, 2003

published by: MensNewsDaily.com

In April of 2002, Palestinian gunmen — who had been involved in a shootout with the Israeli Army — sought refuge by storming into the Church of the Nativity, located in the Israeli city of Bethlehem (currently occupied by the Palestinian Authority). The church is built upon the spot believed to be where the ancient inn and its stable (the historic site of the birth of Jesus) were located. The resulting siege of the church compound lasted approximately 39 days. During negotiations about Israeli presence in Bethlehem, the army withdrew from parts of the city. But, the Israeli Army stood fast to protect the church. After a negotiated settlement, the gunmen were deported to Europe.

Now, the Israeli news service Haaretz is reporting that one of the gunmen has been arrested in Belgium and accused of robberies totaling more than $250,000. It is well known that terrorist cells use robbery as a means of financing their illicit activities. This particular robber is reported to be a member of the member of the Tanzim militia, involved in past incidents of shooting at Israeli cars and the murder of Israeli citizens. Many of the gunmen had been deported to Ireland, but Khalil Mohammed Abdullah al-Nawara had been deported to Belgium.

It appears that — in addition to storming a church— he has no problem with biting the hand that feeds him, because the government of Belgium had provided him with financial assistance and housing. (Please, don't even try to explain to me why any country would do that.) According to the Haaretz report, al-Nawara was initially under guard by Belgian security forces, but this was later lifted after he was deemed not to be a threat to public security.

The robberies against Belgian post offices involved the use of explosives.

Believing that self-avowed terrorists are not a threat to public security is not, unfortunately, the exclusive blunder of neo-socialist European countries. When our US Marines were deployed to Lebanon in 1983, there was an American policy in place that was based on a pretense that terrorists were somehow not dangerous. That policy allowed the car bomber to get close enough to destroy the building where 241 Marines had been living. Many of them were killed while off-duty and resting.

I am directly aware of that policy because, during my security-planning duties in the Air Force, I read an analysis report about the bombing incident. At that time, the report was classified Secret. My understanding is that it was declassified about ten years later. In the past twenty years, I have seen only one fleeting reference to that report in any news article. The report revealed the policy that the Marine sentries were not allowed to have a magazine inserted in their rifles! The time it took for the sentry to take the magazine out of the pouch, insert it in the rifle, jack a round into the chamber, and move the safety off, and then aim his weapon was enough time for the car bomber to gain speed and bypass the sentry post. Someone in our military wrote that policy, and that person — in my opinion — is directly responsible for the deaths of those Marines.

Our military never engaged in a direct retaliation for that bombing. Nor have we ever caught the planners responsible for it, and put them on trial. In any tyrannical culture, signs of weakness are exploited. We were perceived as weak by the Islamists, and we have paid in blood many times for it. (Some modern pundits think that Islamist terrorism began in 1983 in Beirut. Some think it began in 1979 in Tehran. Some think it began in 1972 in Munich. I think that one would have to look a few hundred years prior to the fire-bombing of the Chapel of Saint James in 1925 to find the beginning of Islamist terrorism.) No matter when the wave of terror began, we need to put an end to it.

So, never mind the debates about what we should eat for Christmas. I hope that the government of Belgium will decide to serve up some swift justice.

NOTE 1: When the column below was first published, the editor switched the title and the subtitle. It appears correctly in this book.

NOTE 2: This column is heavily documented via links. Thus, this book cannot convey the full weight of the information. Readers are encouraged to use this column as a springboard for their own research.

NOTE 3: This column has become something of a "classic", in that it has been linked to and quoted by many other writers (often without proper credit). I also link back to it from many of my other columns.

Louder than words

Terrorists' actions — and inactions — reveal true motives

December 29, 2003

published by: MensNewsDaily.com

The material for this article was spawned by an on-air comment that I made recently as a caller to the G. Gordon Liddy talk-radio program. (My semi-frequent calls always begin with, "Mr. Liddy, gung-ho greetings from Nashville!") The host commented that he had not heard this line of thinking anywhere else.

There are several problems with the current War on Terrorism. One of them, by the terrorists' design, is our difficulty in identifying the enemy. This could lead weak people to conclude that we are merely "shadow boxing". And, some of those people with weak convictions will then condemn people with strong convictions.

That leads to a degradation of morale — thus playing into the terrorists' hands.

Another built-in problem is our inability to predict the enemy's target. Until it happened, almost nobody had conceived of the attacks we saw on "9-11". Almost as difficult as determining where terrorists will attack is determining when they will attack. Experienced soldiers will tell you that the hardest part of warfare is quietly waiting for the enemy's next attack.

Then, of course, is the question of "why" they attack. America's "mainstream" news media are straining to pretend that there is no religious element in this war. The same was true ten years ago, when the Liar-In-Chief got our country embroiled in a three-sided religious war in the Balkans. Americans were subjected to a constant overdose of the phrase "ethnic cleansing", with no explanation of how three groups of people — all from the same ethnic stock — could be capable of such a "cleansing". Yes, you read correctly. The Serbs, Croats, and Bosnians are all considered South Slavs. The differences between the three groups are religious. The Serbs are Orthodox Christians, the Croats are Roman Catholic Christians, and the Bosnians are Muslims. Of course, Bill Clinton managed to get American troops into the war to help the only side that is *not* Christian. But, does that actually surprise anyone?

Regardless of the views of the Left (whether from Hollywood or elsewhere), the history of the United States of America is that of a predominantly Christian nation. And, regardless of the complacency of the "mainstream" news media, that is also precisely how the Islamist terrorists view America. That is why, at the terrorist training camps, the targets have crosses on them. They hate us because, as a Christian nation, America is firmly allied with Israel. And, despite the bombast and nitwittery of network TV news, the terrorists are at war with us *because* their god is at war with our God. And — perhaps better than some "average" citizens in this country — the radical Islamists understand the connection between true Christianity and true Judaism. Thus, the radical Islamists viewed their attack upon the World Trade Center as equally an attack upon the large Jewish community in New York City, and an attack upon the larger Christian nation.

But, notably important is where the terrorists did *not* attack.

In the practice of law, there is a doctrine that says, "Silence equals acquiescence". The doctrine is the inverse of the saying "actions speak louder than words". In essence, this doctrine says that "inaction speaks as loudly as action". By their choice of where *not* to attack, the terrorists spoke volumes about their motives.

The Islamist hijackers of "9-11" flew right past the United Nations headquarters, but did not attack it. Both of America's wars in the Persian Gulf region were fought — ostensibly — because of our need to enforce UN resolutions. So, why didn't the terrorists attack the United Nations? Simple: because the UN shares their ideology. (Note that, in this official UN position paper, there is no mention at all of the Mizrahi.)

Most conservative Americans agree that the United Nations is — at its core — profoundly Socialist in nature. As such, it is both anti-American and anti-God. What many well-meaning Americans don't realize is that many Islamic countries, and the Muslim world that they seek to create, are also Socialist in nature. Over a thousand years before Hitler, the Muslims forced Jews to wear a yellow patch on their clothing. There are many other parallels. Like the Fascists and the Communists, both the Muslims and the United Nations share an ultimate goal: world domination. Because of their shared Socialist ideologies, the terrorists did not target their UN enablers.

The Old is New

January 9, 2004

published by: MensNewsDaily.com

This is not an article about the new year; it's about terrorism.

As a culture, we Americans can be a bit short-sighted and impatient. We complain that fast food isn't fast enough. We tend to lose the historical perspective. For example, I know the answer to this question, which baffles most Americans: "How many days were the hostages held at the US Embassy in Tehran, Iran?" It's a very easy number to remember. I also remember what date the embassy was stormed, what day of the week it was, and what other key terrorist event (also by Iranians) happened at the same time.

The point of the above is not to qualify me as a "Jeopardy" contestant. The point is to demonstrate that most Americans don't keep a grip on historical facts, even though they often affect our future. How I wish that Americans could rattle off historical facts the way Joe Sixpack can rattle off sports statistics. (And — unless you're engaged in gambling — sports statistics won't affect your future, anyway.)

As reported recently by WorldNetDaily, our intelligence and security services are worried about a "new" terrorist threat. Apparently, some members of our government are surprised to discover that not all terrorist operatives are Arab males. In our age of "enlightened" equality between the sexes, perhaps those intelligence analysts should be given further "sensitivity training", so that they will come to realize that not all women are made of sugar and spice, etc.

From a more serious angle, though, intelligence analysts need to keep in mind what really motivates our enemies. Ultimately, one of their biggest motivators is envy (see the <u>last five paragraphs</u> of Tammy Bruce's recent MND article for another angle on this). They are powerfully envious of the America that President Reagan called "a shining city upon a hill". It galls Leftist radicals that free citizens can choose their own leaders, and discharge them in an orderly fashion if we are not happy with their performance. Imagine what might have happened with the oil wealth of Iraq if they had this freedom.

Oh, did I say "Leftist radicals"? But, isn't this about terrorism? Read on.

In a recent article, entitled <u>"Louder Than Words"</u>, I demonstrated that the actions of tyrannical regimes and their terrorist henchmen stem from Leftist leanings. The article also described how religious sentiments are inextricably linked to Islamist terrorism. The war of "the prince of this world [system]" (John 12:31) against the "king of all the earth" (Psalm 47:7) is an all-encompassing struggle. Nations are caught in this struggle, and it stretches throughout history. To ignore this fact is to ignore the true root of the problem.

Because deeply-held religious sentiments (which are sometimes different from beliefs, but that's another topic) are at the root of the problem, a purely pragmatic approach to the problem of terrorism will not work. Our country cannot bribe away a lifetime of anticipation of 72 virgins, for example. And, sentiments usually hold even stronger sway with women than they do with men. If a woman grows up in misery and poverty, and is told that killing her "oppressors" will earn her a direct flight to Heaven, then it should not surprise anyone that women have been recruited as suicide bombers.

For this reason, I'm somewhat under-impressed that a Homeland Security intelligence report – titled "Al-Qaida Use of Non-Arab and Female Terror Operatives" – notes that, "Non-Arab al-Qaida operatives could find it easier to avoid unwanted scrutiny since they may not fit typical profiles." Hello! As I wrote in a "9-11" anniversary article, Osama bin-Laden is not a stupid man — he is an evil man. Did our analysts expect the terrorists to wear a uniform? The essence of terrorist operations is to blend in with the target population until the last possible moment before an attack. Therefore, it should not surprise anyone if al-Qaida is actively recruiting blonde-haired, blue-eyed nitwits to join their cause. And, where will they find them? The connections already exist, and have existed for much longer than most people realize.

One of the first modern sources to document the interlocking and cooperative nature of terrorist groups was the 1980 classic, "The Crimson Web of Terror". Disparate groups have pooled their resources to "subvert the dominant paradigm" in various ways for decades. One of the groups at the center of European terrorism in the 1970s was the Baader-Meinhof Gang, which operated in Germany. The group lived on (after the suicides of its founders) as the Red Army Faction (RAF) and attacked the headquarters of the US Air Forces in Europe (USAFE) at Ramstein Air Base. (I was at a briefing about the bombing, back when the information was still classified.) It was well known at that time that European terrorist groups, such as the RAF, were working with the Irish Republican Army (IRA) and their splinters; and, that both of those umbrella groups were training at camps in scattered locations across North Africa. Those camps, of course, were operated by Islamist terror groups, such as the groups headed by Abu Abbas and Abu Nidal. Certain countries — notably Libya, Chad, and Sudan — were supportive of those training camps.

Most people, even if they are fairly well-informed on terrorism, think that such cooperation started about twenty years ago. There are indications, however, that IRA groups secretly cooperated with the Nazis during World War Two, because they viewed a Nazi defeat of the British as a means of freeing Ireland from British rule. (The famous Arab proverb, "The enemy of my enemy is my friend," would apply in that case.) Twenty years ago, I was aware of this connection, but — until now — I have not had unclassified sources available to support my assertion. According to the news account linked above, the British government had just declassified the two files on that topic about six weeks ago.

Most news outlets downplay the role of women in terrorism, and the fact that it has a long history. You see, the commission of heinous acts by female terrorist operatives — who would be considered "empowered" by their culture's standards — does not come across well in newsrooms that support the "empowerment" of women. Another point that does not play well in Left-leaning newsrooms is the concept that women terrorists, like women in general, tend to base decisions on emotions of the moment. Thus, in the eyes of a female terrorist leader, burning down a department store is a suitable response to a police shooting. (Did they fail to honor her expired coupon the week before?) The absolute lack of logic in such a decision is frightening — both to an anti-terrorist planner, and to a pro-feminist editor, but for vastly different reasons. Thus, even our own government's analysts are apparently taken by surprise when the idea of a female operative is considered. The surprise was apparently so great that a special report had to be issued. And — despite having sections entitled "Understanding the Threat" and "The Blind Spots of Terrorism" — there is no word of the special role of female operatives in this statement to the "9-11" Commission.

Clearly, both political and operational leaders in the War Against Terrorism (WAT) need to expand their thinking beyond the "traditional" expectations of conventional security planning. Long before people grow up into such leadership roles, they have been thoroughly indoctrinated into the emotion-based concept that all women are "sugar and spice, and everything nice". Such an adjustment in thinking is not a new requirement. For example, it took many robberies before US law enforcement officials during the Great Depression finally realized that Bonnie Parker was the partner — not the hostage — of Clyde Barrow. Once that realization was made, it wasn't long before "Bonnie and Clyde" met their end in an ambush that involved shotguns and machineguns. Photos of the blood-splashed car served as a crime deterrent for years afterward. Our government needs to revive the type of thinking that stopped Bonnie and Clyde.

Oh, by the way, for those of you that are wondering about the "trivia" question in the opening paragraph: The US Embassy in Tehran was stormed by state-supported college radicals on 04 November 1979. Here in the States, that was a Sunday, and it happened around noon Eastern Time. (Was it timed to insult American Christians, who were just getting out of church at that time? Probably.) The hostages were held for 444 days, ending during the inauguration speech of President Ronald Reagan on 20 January 1981. (See my unpublished article, "The Couric Lie", for more about the timing of the hostage release.) And, at the same time as the storming of the embassy, Iranian nationals stormed the torch of the Statue of Liberty, and burned an American flag (after the news helicopters showed up, of course). That is why no one is allowed to go up into the torch anymore, to this day. I can rattle off those facts any time, day or night, because America's security is more important to me than sports statistics. That's why, apparently, some of our government's analysts think the old is new. For me, the "new" is obviously the same old thing.

Now, what will we do about it?

NOTE: The next two columns are, technically, not about terrorism. But, they belong in this section — precisely because it was my background in studying terrorism that proved that the incident was *not* an act of terrorism. Part Two shows that even experts can miss things.

Nashville Bombing: Details Sketchy, But Emerging

July 24, 2004

Men's News Daily exclusive

Early local news reports about a vehicle bombing in Nashville, TN, contained inaccuracies. But, details are still unclear — both for investigators and the family.

In a Thursday press conference, spokesmen for the Metro Nashville Police Department (MNPD) and the US Bureau of Alcohol, Tobacco, Firearms, and Explosives (ATF) told reporters that "all options are still open". This meant that the incident has not yet been categorized as a homicide, suicide, or accident. Several leads are being pursued.

At approximately 2349 hours (11:49pm) on Tuesday, 20 July, an explosion destroyed a 2001 Land Rover. The owner of the vehicle, William Glenn Young, age 43, was killed in the blast, and his body was apparently thrown through the windshield. Young was alone at the time. The vehicle was parked in an outlying area of the Gaylord

Opryland Resort and Convention Center. The Opryland is an enormous hotel complex, with over two thousand rooms. The vehicle was parked adjacent to a group of construction trailers, which were in the corner of the parking lot. Olympian Construction Company of Nashville was using the lot corner as a staging area for a remodeling project in one of the hotel's many restaurants. An initial police news release described the blast as "massive".

An official spokeswoman for the Opryland Hotel declined to say if Young had been a guest at the hotel, citing standard policy for all guests' privacy. Hotel guest Bonnie McIntosh — vacationing from Charlotte, NC — had arrived in her room minutes before the explosion. She was relaxing before going to bed, and was looking out onto the parking lot. Even though she was looking in the direction of the blast, she did not see anything. But, the window of her fifth-floor room vibrated, and she said the noise was much louder than any explosion that she had ever heard before. The hotel building is about a half-mile from the blast site.

The incident is being investigated by MNPD as a homicide, with assistance from ATF and FBI agents. Special Agent Doug Riggin said that the FBI has ruled out terrorism as a cause for the blast, but declined to specify any facts to support that decision. An ATF spokesman, Special Agent Eric Kehn (pronounced "keen"), confirmed this writer's personal observations of the scene by stating that it was a "high-detonation explosive". In an exclusive conversation with another Federal agent, details of this writer's observations were confirmed as being *exclusive* to high explosives.

That fact conflicts with early local news reports about a "homemade pipe bomb". Homemade bombs normally contain low-order explosives, such as gunpowder or ammonium nitrate.

Although investigators are tight-lipped about this point, the presence of high-order explosives raises the question of a "professional hit". In an exclusive interview at the crime scene, a Federal agent did rule out speculation of Young being the target of a jealous husband or boyfriend. And, there is no apparent connection between Young and the blast location. This combination of facts raises more questions than answers. The same is true of local news interviews with Young's neighbors, who gave conflicting opinions about his personality and employment situation.

In an exclusive interview, a spokesman for the family (identity withheld at this time) described the bomb victim as, "… a genius … just a flat-out genius," and said that Young was an electrical engineer. When asked about local news quotes that Young was "weird", the spokesman said, "I've known a number of highly intelligent people, and I've never known one that wasn't just a little bit weird. Others just don't understand them."

The spokesman also said that the family had been given little information about the incident, and expressed irritation that they learned most of what they knew had come from news accounts that a relative sent to them via Internet. "I thought they were supposed to withhold the name until the victim's family has been contacted."

The spokesman also said that investigators asked Mrs. Young some questions, but mostly just asked for permission to search the house and various cabinets in the home. The victim's wife and son were on vacation at the time of the explosion, thus raising other questions. Agents phoned Mrs. Young several times while she was at the vacation spot. Some of the calls were made by an agent inside her house during the search.

One fact became clear during a Thursday afternoon MND exclusive view of the crime scene. Sometime after the morning press conference, the vehicle had been turned onto its side. Thus, the interior of the vehicle became visible from outside the perimeter of the crime scene. When viewed from one particular angle, it became obvious that the explosion had cleanly cut through a portion of the Land Rover's *frame*. That type of vehicle enjoys a decades-long reputation as one of the toughest off-road vehicles in the world; thus, it has a very solid frame. The cut was about an inch wide, and resembled a cut made with a torch. This type of blast damage suggests a military-grade device, rather than explosives commonly available to or manufactured by everyday civilians. And, the cut in the frame was only visible because of a neatly-shaped hole in the Land Rover's floor. The agent on scene in this exclusive interview refused to confirm or deny the presence of det-cord or any type of "shaped charge", but did agree with this writer's speculation about the placement of the device at the bottom rear of the driver's seat. Other on-scene observations include the fact that the vehicle's roof — which was set aside in the parking lot — was relatively intact. But, the *tops* of the vehicle's windshield pillars were obviously blown *forward*. (As opposed to the entire pillar being bent forward.) That exclusive on-scene observation, coupled with on-scene reports to TV-2 about the location and condition of the windshield, indicate the possibility of a secondary cutting charge along the vehicle's forward interior roofline. The presence of such a secondary charge would confirm a carefully planned bombing.

The effect of a cutting charge on the roofline would be to provide a directed ventilation of blast energy. Such a cut could be achieved with det-cord. Upward blast ventilation would be consistent with on-scene reports about the trajectory of the victim's body from the vehicle. (Those details are being withheld by MND at this time, pending the family's viewing of the body, and the release of preliminary findings from the Medical Examiner.) Such an upward ventilation of blast energy would also explain why the center of the vehicle was destroyed, and the back wheels blown completely off, but everything forward of the windshield was nearly untouched. Upward ventilation would also explain why the Land Rover's fuel tank appeared to be mostly intact, despite being inches from the neatly-shaped hole in the vehicle's floor. The interior of the vehicle was burned so badly that some of the metal's coatings were ashen-white. Blast ventilation can provide extra oxygen to the initial fireball.

Upward ventilation of the blast would also explain why — despite the obvious power of the explosion, which was heard and felt miles away — the vehicle remained in place and the shell remained intact. Without such ventilation, certain parts of the vehicle would likely have been spread out in the parking lot. Some of the ventilating effect can be explained by the windows and windshield. But, in this writer's opinion, those factors do not explain all of the ventilation of this particular blast.

Both at the press conference and around the crime scene, agents specified that the Land Rover company had been very cooperative. The company provided a similar vehicle, and two technicians, to give comparative analysis of the damaged Rover and its debris. A report by the local newspaper, The Tennessean, inaccurately reported that the ATF had purchased the vehicle. In fact, the Land Rover company made the vehicle available to investigators free of charge.

The blast location was in an area that is distant enough from any business or residence to ensure that no bystanders were injured. But, the area is also visible to passersby, especially from the tourist area of adjacent Music Valley Drive. There, several bars close on weekdays around midnight — virtually guaranteeing that the incident would be reported to the fire department immediately. (And, thus, minimizing collateral damage to property of Opryland or the construction company.) The side of the parking lot facing the Opryland Hotel is lined with a thick grove of trees. That treeline extends past the on-site childcare center for hotel employees. Because of the late hour, neither children nor staff were in any danger at the time of the blast; and, the facility provided shielding from the blast for any strolling hotel guests. Likewise, the vehicle was positioned among the construction trailers in such a way that the trailers could've provided a cushioning effect, and much of the blast energy deflected upward. It appears that someone went to great lengths to ensure that only the bombing victim would be harmed. Some might say that the preparations approach the level of "genius".

Local news reports indicate that the family declared bankruptcy one year ago. But, a neighbor interviewed by several news outlets indicated that Young had just landed a business contract involving high pay and international travel, possibly in Nicaragua. Nashville police would like to speak with anyone that may have spoken with William Young in recent weeks, especially in the week preceding the bombing, to determine his state of mind. Anyone having information about the incident is asked to contact the Nashville police at (615) 74-CRIME, or send a message via the ATF Web site.

The conflicting facts of this story create more questions than answers. Was the death of William G. Young an elaborate suicide, capitalizing on fears of terrorism to cover up his true motive? Or, did another person lure Young to a visible, but safe, spot to prevent him from conducting unspecified business in another country? Was the story about the contract true, or a smokescreen? If true, then, was Young's international business in any way related to intelligence activity and/or the War Against Terrorism? Is there any chance that the bombing was a case of "mistaken identity"? (Independent research by Men's News Daily revealed that the victim has the same name as the Federal judge that is hearing the case of alleged "shoe bomber" Richard Reid.) Was there a hidden connection between Young and the blast location? Details remain sketchy, but the mystery is expected to unravel further, beginning sometime after the family's Friday meeting with the Medical Examiner.

Nashville Bombing:
MND Finds New Evidence at Scene

July 30, 2004

Men's News Daily exclusive

In the previous MND article on the recent bombing incident in Nashville, a Federal agent had confirmed this writer's analysis of the vehicle's burned-out shell. That analysis was that the primary explosive device was a high-order explosive; and, that the device was placed at the right-rear-bottom corner of the driver's seat. Now, an exclusive Men's News Daily examination of the crime scene has turned up key physical evidence that police officers, detectives, bomb-squad members, and Federal agents apparently overlooked.

The remains of the vehicle were removed sometime after MND last visited the crime scene on the afternoon of Thursday, 22 July. When a camera crew from WKRN TV-2 went to the scene early that evening (to take video of the vehicle's cleanly-cut frame, which MND had alerted the station to), the vehicle remains were already gone. The crime scene was cleared the following morning.

On the afternoon of Thursday, 29 July, this writer returned to the scene to take a look around, now that the area was freely accessible. A supervisor from the electrical sub-contractor for the construction site gave this writer permission to go anywhere in the vicinity, including to climb atop the office-trailer. The bombed vehicle had been parked adjacent to the electrical company's trailer, which sustained minor blast damage. The supervisor also stated that a clean-up contractor had washed down the trailer's exterior, along with other areas of the crime scene. He further stated that the contractor had been retained by the Opryland Hotel, owner of the parking lot where the bombing occurred.

    Because the scene had been cleared by police, and permission had been obtained from the on-scene site supervisor, any debris found at the scene would be "fair game" for this exclusive examination. This writer climbed atop the office-trailer, and found several pieces of vehicle parts, along with glass fragments and charred bits of asphalt. Other evidence viewed at the scene — both in this examination and the previous one — suggest that the powerful blast was ventilated upwards.

    Damage done to a pickup truck, which the bombed vehicle had been parked next to, shows that the explosion's significant power had been contained to a fairly small circle around the victim's vehicle. Among that evidence, the outer half of the pickup's right-front tire had been flash-charred, but the inner half of the tire retained the normal suppleness of rubber. And, the charring was in an arc pattern, showing the actual shape of the fireball that radiated from the blast. (In fact, not even the entire outer portion of the tire had been charred.) The fireball had been hot enough to burn the asphalt, but left unscarred portions where the target vehicle's wheels had fallen to the pavement. The burn pattern on the pavement indicates that the rims had already been blown off the wheels, allowing them to hit the ground. (That is consistent with this writer's previous observations of the vehicle. The wheel lugs were bent, and the rims were missing.)

On top of the trailer, this writer found several fragments, which were later identified to be consistent with a 2001 Land Rover Discovery, like the target vehicle. Also found on top of the trailer was a small evidence flag, indicating that someone from the police had been on top of the trailer during the investigation. (Or, that the flag had been tossed up there at some point.) This writer gathered the fragments, and took them to the same two Land Rover technicians that had assisted Federal agents at the scene.

Most of the fragments were of no major consequence, having come from parts of the vehicle that would be expected to come loose in a blast. But, one small metal bracket was of interest. The bracket was two-layered, and showed the same type of clean-cut blast damage as the frame observed by this writer during the previous examination. The bracket was identified as coming from the right-rear-bottom corner of the front seat frame. The technician explained that, in that model of Land Rover, both front seats are identical. Thus, there was theoretically no way to determine which front seat the bracket came from. But, the type of blast damage indicates that it was close to the source of the explosion. And, the corner of the seat frame is the same corner where a Federal agent confirmed last week as the area where the bomb was planted behind the driver's seat. So, the bracket most likely came from the driver's seat.

Once these facts were confirmed by the Land Rover technicians, it became apparent that the metal bracket could be a significant piece of evidence. This writer contacted the Metro Nashville Police Department (MNPD), and spoke with a homicide detective. The detective made arrangements for an officer from the Mobile Crime Scene Unit to pick up the bracket. The officer expressed surprise at the discovery of the bracket, and noted the location of its discovery. He stated that it would be turned over to the ATF for lab analysis, to determine if there is any residue on the bracket. The residue could help investigators to specify the type of explosive that was used.

On Wednesday, the MNPD Public Affairs Section told Men's News Daily that there were no new details available for release. Multiple attempts, over several days, have not resulted in any follow-up interviews with the victim's family. For the past two days, the home phone was not answered. Calls to the cell phone number now result in a recording that it is not a working number. Men's News Daily will continue to follow leads on this story, because unconfirmed reports point to the existence of other new evidence. If the evidence is confirmed, it could explain the motive for the bombing.

NOTE: The Medical Examiner's Office never released the details of the examination. But, a police source told me that a suicide note was found later. When I returned to the family's home for confirmation of any details, Mrs. Young refused to answer the door (once she saw who I was through the window.) This information was not enough for a new column; so, there never was a Part Three.

Section 4

Politics

Part A

Wesley Clark

The Evil We've Been Spared

War and Politics

December 31, 2003

There is a great line from a popular Christian song: "Prayer Warrior", by Twila Paris. The line says, "We may never know the evil we've been spared."

In an unpublished article about the 2003 TV premiere week (before I joined Mens' News Daily), one of the shows that I featured was "Threat Matrix". That show features stories "ripped from the headlines". The recurring theme of the show is that the general public will never know the evil that we've been spared, thanks to the work of this team of super secret agents.

Real teams of agents, investigators, analysts, and patrolmen work every day — both overtly and covertly — to protect America. They work for many of the "alphabet soup" Federal agencies — plus state, county, and local police departments, and many private security companies. Some of their work is necessarily secret. Some of it comes to the surface. Sometimes, a "routine" incident can have other hidden factors, which might lead to terrorism. (The driver in this taxi crash was going about 100mph into a convenience-store parking lot, missed a gasoline pump by two or three feet, went airborne, and his car impacted a sign pole about six feet off the ground. I personally observed the front section of the car's frame wrapped completely around the metal pole. A witness at the scene told me that the driver, a Nigerian national, had at least one bullet wound when he was put in the ambulance. The medical examiner's office never returned my call for confirmation and further information.)

In a press event in Nashville on Tuesday, retired Army four-star general Wesley Clark made one of the most ridiculous statements in modern political history. This man, who definitely should have known better, actually stated about the War on Terrorism, "...we didn't have to fight [the war] didn't have anything to do with Osama Bin Laden ...."

Hello! (note the date)

[NOTE: The above link was to a Defense Department news release from October of 2001, in which Secretary Rumsfeld said that it might take a long time to find Osama bin-Laden.]

This is not just any presidential candidate; although, I would hope that any candidate would have the good sense to check his information before such a speech. This is a man that had been the Supreme Commander of NATO. Even in the public news reports, we saw that our forces were involved in cave-clearing operations, in search of bin-Laden's elusive al-Qaida. Imagine how much more information General Clark can access; but, he chose to make such an outlandish statement. What reason could this "other man from Little Rock" have for attempting to mislead voters?

Political analysts have speculated that General Clark is actually the point-man for another secret operation: the "non-campaign" of Hillary Clinton for the presidency. Will Clark throw himself on a political land mine to pave the way for Hillary's juggernaut? If so, will he be rewarded with the job of Secretary of Defense? If so, would he commit the will and resources necessary to defend America? Would he have the will to take the war to the doorstep of the terrorists? If Hillary is elected president, would she bring back Janet Reno as attorney general? Considering the well-known Clinton "loathing" of the military, what would happen to our military budget under Hillary and/or Clark? What would happen to the budgets for all those agents, investigators, analysts, and patrolmen? What will (or, more correctly, won't) happen to Osama bin-Laden?

In one of the greatest exercises of individual power in history, American voters will go to the polls next November and choose the next President of the United States. Much blood has been shed to maintain that right, and to shine freedom's light to the rest of the world. We can choose a president that thinks America is worth fighting for; or, we can choose a former general that doesn't seem to think so. To me, the choice is obvious.

And, hopefully, we'll realize the evil we've been spared.

Wesley Clark: Discharge Immediately!

February 7, 2004

MensNewsDaily.com exclusive commentary

Tennessee is being invaded, and a retired general wants to lead the invasion. Rather than give this general a promotion to President of the United States, my advice is that the citizens should discharge him from the campaign immediately.

Don't worry, I'm not preparing to mount a Walking Horse and go striding from Bristol to Memphis, shouting, "The Leftists are coming! The Leftists are coming!" (It is quite tempting; but, any excuse to ride a horse is a good one.)

Nope — the invasion to which I refer will come in the form of Democratic presidential candidates. They will come in flanked by assistants of various types. They will come in talking about values. (But, whose values?) They will come in talking about tradition. (Waving a flag?) They will come in talking about jobs. (Only union jobs, of course.) They will come in kissing children (if they live). They will come in trying to win votes from veterans. (Inspect closely.) One candidate, however, will be absent from the pack. Apparently, Howard Dean believes that Wisconsin is more important than Tennessee. (And, how many US Presidents have come from Wisconsin?)

As a side note, my guess is that Howard Dean is relying upon the endorsement of Al Gore to win him votes in Tennessee. But, if **Al Gore's endorsement of Al Gore** didn't work in 2000, why would it work for Howard Dean in 2004? Oh, but I forgot, I'm not an "enlightened" member of the "in-crowd". If I was, then I would know that campaign dollars and "who you know" are more important than beliefs, integrity, and experience. And, there is a well-funded new voice for members of the in-crowd: the Music Row Democrats. Their stated goal is to "dispel the notion that all country music people are Republican". (But, by their very existence, they prove that at least one section of the entertainment world is not in the grip of the Left.) Those who earn huge salaries off the work of conservative-minded musicians, and then spend big money on Leftist causes, are the people I was talking about when I referred to "suits" in my recent article about the desecration of the American flag at the Super Bowl. (Of course, this paragraph could be the wooden stake through the heart of my hopes of making money as a lyricist.) Back to the point of this side note, Dean can only snub Tennessee at his political peril. To his credit, General Clark understands that strategic fact.

My primary concern in this article is with the candidacy of Wesley Clark, because he projects the type of image that many Southern Democrats might buy. Tall, handsome, well-spoken, and with a high-ranking retirement — these are qualities that voters looking on the surface might wrongly equate with another former general: President Andrew Jackson of Tennessee. One of the problems with the current state of politics in America is that most voters only scan the surface. And, on the surface, Wesley Clark looks very good. (But, on the surface, nobody could find Saddam Hussein living in a septic tank.)

Here's what one finds beneath the surface regarding Wesley Clark.

Myth #1: "He is qualified to be president, because he is a Rhodes scholar." This statement is an oxymoron, because anyone that graduates the Oxford program named after Cecil Rhodes should be **automatically disqualified** from any leadership position of any kind within the United States of America. The essential mission of the Rhodes scholarship program is to plant the seeds of Socialism into otherwise bright young minds. And, never was the planting of those seeds so successful as when Bill Clinton (another Rhodes scholar) implemented one Communist policy after another during his presidency. Clinton surrounded himself with people from Little Rock, and Wesley Clark was part of that inner circle. To think that Wesley Clark will not have at least one Clinton (most likely two) on his Cabinet would be foolish. It would be as foolish as a conclusion that another member of the Little Rock circle, Vince Foster, committed suicide. Now, given that Bill Clinton shredded much of the American military, what do you think would happen to the military with a Clinton understudy as president? And, what position do you think that the "honorable" former President Bill "loathing the military" Clinton would occupy in the Cabinet? (Secretary of Defense?! Attorney General??)

Myth #2: "He is qualified to be president, because he is a retired general." This is a trickier myth to unravel, because I do believe that military leadership experience is *usually* a qualifier for political leadership. But, there are definitely exceptions. It seems that, when looking into the background of General Clark, there are two types of quotes available. One type is a quote from people that adore him; the other is a quote from people that despise him. I haven't seen many quotes in between. Clark is portraying himself as a "centrist" (just as Bill Clinton did). But, his persona is apparently quite polarizing. This is a contradiction, as are many of the things I've seen about Clark's background. (Admittedly, some people might say some of these same things about me. But, I'm not running for president, and I'm not one to dodge issues — even unpleasant ones.) Something else to consider is the source of the comments. Positive comments are often made by people that have never been in the military, and who key in on the "snapshot" quotes (from his military record) put out by the Clark campaign. (Of course, one of the most glowing quotes came from Alexander "I'm in charge" Haig. So, it is a bit suspect in my mind.) Negative comments are often made by people that were also career military; and, in some cases, have had to live with the effects of some of Clark's orders. (And, the Secretary of Defense that fired Clark said, "…the ax, as such, when it fell spoke for itself.") So, in my view, the negative comments that I've seen carry a lot more weight. (Note: to be balanced, it should be noted that Col. Hackworth later praised Clark, after he became a candidate. But, the archives of Hackworth's columns indicate that he had written more than one rather negative article about Clark. It will be hard to recover from a man of Col. Hackworth's caliber **calling Clark "The Ultimate Perfumed Prince"**. And, the tone of "Reporting for duty: Wesley Clark" seems to be as much anti-"Dubya" as it is pro-Clark. But, should we replace a winning wartime president with someone like Clark? Not in my opinion.)

As my regular readers know, I want my opinions to be as fully-informed as possible. Although I look at things from the political Right, that does not mean that I don't pay attention to the political Left. (The reason my opinions are on the Right is *because* I've read plenty of material from the Left.) Oddly, there are many Left-wing Democrats that are referring to Clark as a war criminal. (Many of the sources for those accusations come from openly Socialist sources, which one would expect to support another Rhodes scholar for president.) Serious accusations that Clark may have approved the specific bombing of civilian targets seem to overlooked by the same liberal media that has given Clark so much exposure. I know that exposure on network TV can make even a bad officer look good. (During the TV coverage of Operation Iraqi Freedom, I sent an e-mail to another network about a credibility problem with their employment of a certain retired general. After my message, that general was never seen on TV again.) A signal quality of bad officership is to flip-flop on your positions. Another quality of bad officership is the willingness to support a clearly immoral policy. It would appear that one immoral campaign led to another. (And, it is not a recovery to state, "Belgrade was bombed on both Easters.") As I've written before, the war in the Balkans was a three-sided religious war, with <u>Bill Clinton supporting the only non-Christian side in the war</u>.

Clark's campaign ads say he will get us out of Iraq, but there is no mention of Bosnia or Haiti, which Clinton got us into without any justification. So, as you can see, a lengthy military career is not an automatic certificate of qualification for political leadership. <u>(And, most Democratic candidates don't speak at Republican dinners.)</u> No matter where one lands on the political spectrum, <u>it helps to follow the campaign laws</u>.

Myth # 3: "<u>Clark is qualified to be president, because he is bipartisan</u>." There is an old saying, "If you don't stand for something, then you'll fall for anything." I think this saying best sums up the "bipartisan" quality of Wesley Clark. Some people view the word "bipartisan" as signifying a good negotiator. Other people view the word "bipartisan" as signifying someone with no core values. I view Clark's version of "bipartisan" as someone that will go "all over the map" to reach the ultimate goal. And, just what is Clark's ultimate goal? Go back to the fact that he is a Rhodes scholar, and the ultimate goal of Cecil Rhodes: a global Socialist government, ruled by graduates of his program. Members of the Rhodes fellowship see themselves as a separate class of people, destined to rule over us common folk. <u>Clark was born a Jew, raised as a Baptist, and became a Catholic</u>. He has heaped praise on Republicans for years, but is running for president as a Democrat. Other than the dedication to world Socialism that undergirds the Rhodes program, **what does Wesley Clark really stand for?** Is he a true "bipartisan" negotiator;

or, is he simply an "unhinged" power-grabber? Is he a commanding presence on the political battlefield, or a puppet of the Clintonista machine? If he gets elected, will he appoint Bill Clinton to his Cabinet? If he becomes the Democratic candidate, would Hillary Clinton be his running mate? And, if Clark is elected president, would he ultimately end up like another apparent "bipartisan" figure — Vince Foster?

Months before the presidential primary season began, an article about Clark's entry into the race seems to have summed up his campaign potential. The article in the Christian Science Monitor quoted a political analyst as saying, "Someone has to be the anti-Dean...." And, with the revelation of a smoldering feud between Al Gore and the Clintons, it appears to me that Dean and Clark are both proxy soldiers in that feud. Now, does that sound like someone that you'd want to be your next president?

NOTE: Three days after this column was published, Wesley Clark suddenly and unexpectedly **withdrew from the presidential race**.

Part B

Hillary Clinton

War as Backdrop

War and politics — Part Two

[NOTE: Part One was "The Evil We've Been Spared"]

December 24, 2003

published by: MensNewsDaily.com

In part one of this series, we saw that Saddam Hussein has handed the 2004 election to the Bush-Cheney ticket ... in a briefcase.

When I was a boy, my father taught me a saying that, "It takes a Democrat to get America into a war, and it takes a Republican to get us out of it." The amazing part was that my father, like most of my family, was a life-long Democrat. But, many life-long Democrats are very conservative at heart. They have been misled to think that the Democratic Party is "for the people". As we will see in part three of this series, much of what is said by Democratic Party leaders has a separate set of definitions. Yes, those leaders are for "the people" — they are for only the people in their proletariat circle.

One cannot find a more quintessential example than the recent "visit with the troops" in Afghanistan by the junior US Senator from New York. It still astounds me that a freshman senator — who not only has no military background, nor connections, but has the same loathing for the military as her husband — has managed to worm her way onto the Armed Services Committee. Thus, it was impossible for anyone in the military to say "no" to her plans for a photo-op with the troops during Thanksgiving stops in Afghanistan and Iraq. Due to long friendships with members of the Hollywood Left, both Bill and Hillary Clinton are quite familiar with the importance of camera angles to political success.

So, conveniently, Hillary used the war as a backdrop (including bulletholes).

She was far from alone in her use of that strategy, even though she was nearly alone at the table in the mess hall. Even the briefest news clips showed that there were more reporters at her table than soldiers. Favorable news reports said that "more than a dozen soldiers" had their photos taken with Hillary. Remember, those troops (and their commanders) knew in advance that she was coming. A recent caller to a talk-radio show said that he was there, and that officers had to order troops to line up with her. By contrast, President Bush appeared by surprise, and he was surrounded by hundreds of cheering troops. And, revealingly, President Bush served the troops, but Senator Clinton bumped ahead in line to be served by the troops. Many years before he became the Commander-in-Chief, George W. Bush had served under others in uniform. He knows which way to turn when the music plays. And, by the strategies he has approved, it is obvious that he also knows which end of the tube the round comes from.

Of course, the political visits to the Middle East took a back seat to the recent capture of Saddam Hussein. When he was found, hiding in a cold septic tank, the contrast could not have been more understated, as one of our special operators said simply, "Warm regards from President Bush." The effect was priceless.

Immediately in the wake of the news of this military and intelligence victory, however, the spinmeisters of the Leftist Media turned the story's focus to that of the Democratic challengers and the 2004 presidential election. I'm sure that it would also be possible for the Media Elite to turn a story about a prom night car accident into a forum about Democratic challengers and the presidential election. Constantly interspersed between facts about the capture, Dan Rather kept making comments about the effect of this incident on the Democratic challengers. (One would think the effect would be on the current occupant of the White House; but, apparently that was not considered news.)

In particular, Rather gave an opportunity for a lengthy soliloquy to Senator John Kerry. He used that opportunity as a pitch for globalism, using such buzz-phrases as, "We should bring the world to the table..." Kerry also launched an attack by saying, "We should get other countries to share the costs and burdens of the War Against Terrorism...." Hello! According to a recent Pentagon briefing, we have about 34 other countries helping in Iraq, and 27 countries helping in Afghanistan. (Some of those countries overlap, but not all. A safe estimate is probably 40 different countries helping us in the War Against Terrorism.) But, of course, Senator Kerry made his comment in such a tone as to make it sound as though President Bush had not done enough to enlist the help of other

133

countries. The reality is that he has done a tremendous job, even bringing in countries that were not only our former enemies, but enemies with each other. (For example, there is a centuries-old cultural rivalry between Russia and Ukraine. The president has been able to capitalize on that in a unique way. More on that in a future article.) To listen to the **Nay-saying Nine** (and a half), it would sound as though President Bush was making his foreign policy decisions on a whim. It sounds to me like the real whim is in how to attack that policy.

Within minutes of the Kerry interview, CBS reporter Kimberly Dozier, broadcasting live from Iraq, was asked by Rather if she had any reactions from Iraqi citizens. Dozier replied that Iraqis had avoided interviews because, "It was the arrest of one of their symbols." Hello! Is she talking about the same "symbol" that threw people into shredders? (If she knew anything about Middle Eastern culture, then she would realize that the *real* symbol was that little boy, riding on Saddam's toppled statue, beating its face with the bottom of his shoe.) Then, she emphasized that the Iraqis had begun to mistrust Americans. Had it occurred to Dozier that the average Iraqi might be avoiding a televised interview for fear of being killed by Saddam loyalists?! Duh! (I try to avoid using that expression in writing; but, it certainly fits in this application.) It seems to me that Dozier, making such a foolish comment while on occupied foreign soil, came perilously close to "giving aid and comfort to the enemy", which is still an element of the Federal law against treason. Treason is still punishable by death.

Of course, the cake-topper of all foolish comments was that of Howard Dean, who said that the capture of Saddam Hussein had been timed to help President Bush in next year's election. So much has been written about it that there is little left to be said. But, the reality of the capture definitely took the wind out of the Democrats' recent musings about a planned "October surprise" by our current president, George W. Bush.

For those that might not remember, the phrase "October surprise" was used by the Democrats over twenty years ago, when they were stunned by the overwhelming election victory of Ronald Reagan and his running-mate, George H. W. Bush. In the wake of their 1980 defeat, they accused "George the elder" of having engaged in secret negotiations with the Iranian revolutionary government. They were holding Americans hostage, after storming the US Embassy in Tehran on 04 November 1979. The Democrats accused George H. W. Bush, who was Director of Central Intelligence under President Nixon, of having secretly flown to Paris to conduct these alleged negotiations. When confronted by the facts of Mr. Bush's schedule on the day of the alleged act, and the fact that not even the supersonic Concorde airliner could have gotten him there and back in the time alleged, the Democrats simply launched a ludicrous second-wave attack by saying that Mr. Bush had made the trip aboard an SR-71 spy plane. They actually said that, and expected people to believe it. And, people *did* believe it! At the time, George H. W. Bush was in his early sixties. The SR-71 (now retired) flew at the edge of space, at three times the speed of sound. It was buffeted by so much atmospheric friction that the aircraft had to cool down for three hours after it landed before anyone could touch it. But, in typical bombastic fashion, the Democrats wanted the American public to accept their "October surprise" accusations as hard fact. Now that we've examined the truth, who can believe Howard Dean's accusations about the timing of Saddam's capture?

For all of mankind's history, and despite many technological advances, there is one simple word that has been associated with war: fire. Fire produces light and heat. Light separates truth from lies. Heat purifies metal and makes it stronger. In the light that has emanated from this war, the truth of our cause has been revealed. In the heat that has radiated from this war, our country has been forged together and tempered stronger. Any politician that chooses to use war as a backdrop should keep those factors in mind. Any politician that fails to keep them in mind is headed for a "quagmire" and sure defeat.

Staple down the tablecloths!

War and Politics — Part Three

January 6, 2004

MensNewsDaily.com exclusive commentary

In part two of this series, we saw the good and the bad of candidates using war as a backdrop for their campaign photo opportunities. Now, a look at one "campaign".

Silly members of the Leftist news-media elite persist in using the word "if" while discussing Hillary Clinton's role in next year's presidential elections. There is no "if"!! Hillary wants to become the next President of the United States. Look out!

There, I've made my point. (But, please keep reading anyway.)

Thanks to that same news-media elite gang — "the vast left-wing conspiracy", to twist a phrase from my enemy's playbook — most of you now reading this column have probably never heard of a little event in Binghamton, New York, in early May of 1999. The event to which I refer was the very first anti-Hillary rally in NY State. It was only days after she launched her infamous "listening tour". You know, the one in which she had to carry out her "duties" as First Lady. Oddly, although First Lady is a national position (not office), her tour was conducted almost exclusively in New York

State. As I see it, the only real "duty" of the First Lady is conducted somewhere on the second floor of the White House; and, only with her husband. In contrast, Hillary Clinton felt that her "duty" was to be whisked around New York on a tax-funded airplane to meet lots of strangers. Somebody had to stand up and say no, and a rally seemed like the place to do it. I was there, because I organized it. To borrow another phrase — from the famous robot on the *Lost in Space* television series — "Warning, warning! Danger, danger!"

Democrats are finally coming to their senses, led by Zell Miller of Georgia. He has come out and admitted what Bubba Doublewide has secretly known for years: the Democratic Party has been taken over by Communists. Yes, I said Communists. (And, thanks to Bubba, it was the Southern Democrats that helped put Ronald Reagan in the White House in order to stop the Communists. And, he did. Well, overseas, anyway.) Some people have tried to "politely" describe the Clintonistas and their ilk as "Left-wingers" or "Socialists". For those people, I would "politely" point to what Vladimir Lenin said to the news media of his day, shortly after the Bolsheviks secured power: "A socialist **is** a communist." There you have it, straight from the horse's ... uh ... mouth. And, by any accepted definition, the core leadership of the Democratic Party has clearly demonstrated — in word and deed — that they support the Communist agenda.

Modern society is full of "isms", but there are three that have more in common that most people think. They are: communism, globalism, and Islamism. Their common thread is another "ism":

totalitarianism. And, the people that adhere to these "isms" want to help usher in tyranny on a global scale. There are two main ways to stop tyranny: politics (a war of words) and combat (a real war). So, whom are we fighting?

Hillary Clinton is a Communist, and so are some of her close allies. I know more about one in particular, because I've done some focused research. That person is Maurice Hinchey, who was elected to Congress in 1992, after serving for 18 years in the NY State Assembly. I ran against Hinchey in 1994 as a third-party candidate. (Factoid: I was the first person in the history of the United States to run for Congress while working full-time at McDonalds. How that happened is a topic for another time. Many people told me at the time that I was living The American Dream.) Although I lost the election, my average cost-per-vote was only 65 cents! That is one of the most efficient campaigns in modern political history. My strategy was simple: tell the truth. You see where it got me. That is because Communists gain power by very skillful lying, and many voters choose to believe the lie that offers them the greatest "benefit".

Hillary and Hinchey are behind many of the Communist schemes that gurgle through the legislative process — below the radar of most observers. Hinchey is a member of the Progressive Caucus, along with open homosexual Bernie Sanders, who hosts this membership roster. (Is hosting a page for a Communist organization part of the Web-hosting privileges of a Congressman?) Their name implies — on the surface — that they are in favor of progress. Their idea of progress, however, is that of advancing the Bolshevik

Revolution until it smothers what is left of the real America. It may surprise some of you that more than 10 percent of the members of Congress support the Communist ideology.

The above might sound like strong language to some; but, it is only an honest representation of the facts. Strong language is needed in order to overcome the adept use of "smoke and mirrors" by the Communists in our government. But, don't take my word for the connection. Please note Congressman Hinchey's own words, praising the Progressive Caucus and their legislative plan. His words are found in this release from the Communist Party of the USA. Hinchey's quote, like those of other "PC" members (I'm sure the initials are no accident), is laden with buzz-phrases that must be closely scrutinized to extract the true meaning. I've been to enough of Hinchey's public events, and debated him on television, to be able to translate from the Commie-speak. And, I've listened to enough of Hillary's public remarks to know that she uses that same dialect.

Here are some examples of Commie-speak.

"We need to reduce local property taxes." meaning: We want to take over control of all schools by placing them under the US Department of Education. Then, although your Federal taxes will rise astronomically, your local property taxes will go down somewhat. Trust us; we know what's best for you. Besides, it's the economy, stupid! (Isn't it interesting that the most educated citizens in the history of mankind are regarded as being too stupid to decide what's best for our children?)

"We need a fair system of taxation." meaning: We want to buy votes from poor people by promising them a free ride on the backs of rich people. (And, we control the definition of "rich".) By giving them a free ride, we can insure that they will not have any incentive to become rich themselves. If they did, then they might discover how unfair the current (read: Communist) tax system really is. The only fair tax is a flat tax. There is a good reason why Thomas Jefferson said, "The power to tax is the power to destroy." Whenever there is a so-called "progressive" (buzz-word for "Communist") tax, there is no telling what will be taxed next.

"I'm not campaigning for office." meaning: My legal advisors have assured me that, technically, I'm not breaking any campaign laws by going around acting like a candidate, trying to get up enough money to actually become a candidate. It worked for Hillary by "listening" in New York, just as it worked for Jesse Jackson by "helping" in Lebanon in 1983; except, of course, that Hillary's non-campaign actually got her elected. And, just to make sure that Joe Sixpack can't do anything about it, we'll call him a "lobbyist", and handcuff him with "campaign reform".

"I support the military." meaning: Note that this phrase does not specify *our* military. It is used by Communists that support putting the military of the United States under the command of the United Nations. It is the grammatical parallel of saying, "I did not have sex with *that* woman, Miss Lewinsky, (looking into the camera, and speaking to Monica about another woman in the room)" versus,

"I did not have sex with that woman: *Miss Lewinsky*." Like most Leftist ideas, "the devil is in the details".

"After all, it's for the children." meaning: This is one of the most effective, and heinous, of the Commie-speak buzz-phrases. What it really means is, "Ha! We have you over a barrel, you complacent saps! You don't even know *what* we're trying to sneak through, much less how to stop it. But, even if you get up the gumption to try, we will make you look like monsters in the public arena, because you will be perceived as doing something bad to children." Here's an example. If you support gun ownership in order to protect your family, we'll make you look as though you support the wackos that shot up Columbine High School. After all, disarming the public (so they can't resist tyranny") is "for the children". Of course, you have to use their definition of "children". Remember "Mister Ponytail" at the 1992 presidential debates? He pleaded for Bill Clinton to, "Just treat us as your children." And, he did. God help us.

We have all heard and read these buzz-phrases many times; but, have we truly listened? Apparently not, or the Clintons would have been given "new employment horizons" back in 1996. Those same buzz-phrases have been used by Leftist candidates at nearly every level of government, all across America, for many years. The phrases sound innocent, but the meaning behind them is grossly malevolent.

In an effort to look as innocent as they sound, Leftist candidates have a penchant for using the public schools as a backdrop for their campaign TV ads. I believe that, if private citizens would do their research (as I did when living in NY State), they would find that most states prohibit the use of school facilities for partisan political purposes. But, the Communists that control the Democratic Party have such a stranglehold on our school systems that they do it with impunity, and with regularity. As a private citizen, in 1998, I filed a pro se lawsuit against Congressman Hinchey to stop him from airing the ads. One of the co-defendants was Judith Hope, a close friend of Hillary's from Little Rock, who moved to New York to take over the state's Democratic Party a few years in advance of Hillary's "spontaneous" campaign for the US Senate. What a coincidence.

Please pardon the length of that foundational digression, but it was necessary in order to demonstrate that "Commie-speak" exists for specific reasons. Those reasons are designed to obfuscate the true motives of the candidates and their organizations. Without such smokescreens, the Communists among us know that the average American would stand up and put a stop to their activities. But, by skillfully weaving their lies, the Communists among us have gained significant power. And, now that the ideological Communists have gone "mainstream", they are in a position to help the people that helped to put them there. One of the key groups that helped the Communists hijack America is the organized homosexual lobby. If you don't believe that there is a connection between homosexuals and communism, then you probably don't know about the Mattachine Society. <u>They were hard-core Communists that happened to also be homosexual activists.</u> They did much of their work as secretly as possible. And, they banded together to fight for all of their Leftist, anti-God causes. That is why <u>homosexuals support pro-abortion causes,</u> even though homosexuals (by definition) do not create babies. And, that is why there was a pro-lesbian rally in DC on Inauguration Day in 1993 to properly recognize and thank Communists such as Hillary Clinton. (Audiotapes of the rally were aired on The Rush Limbaugh Show. One speaker shouted into the microphone, "Finally, we have a First Lady that we can f---!)

    This article barely scratches the surface of showing just how dangerous Hillary would be if she ever resumes her occupation of (not merely "occupancy in") the White House. Remember that, as they exited from power, the Clintonista Gang literally stole many items from the White House and its environs. The category of stolen property that stands out in everyone's memory is the silverware. Well, if you ever see Hillary Clinton occupying the White House again, my suggestion is that you staple down the tablecloths.

STOP Hillary NOW!!

May 11, 2006

published by: RenewAmerica.us

Since 1993, when she tried to become the *tzarina* of government-sponsored health care, I have suspected that Hillary Clinton wanted to become the President of the United States. Since the mid-1990s — when one of her best friends, Judith Hope, moved from Little Rock to New York, and then "suddenly" became the chairman of the NY Democratic Party — I was confident that the fix was in. Since 1999, when she bilked the taxpayers in a phony "listening tour" scam to launch her campaign, there was no doubt in my mind that Mrs. Clinton was going to use a run for the US Senate as a stepping stone toward the Oval Office. Now, in 2006, the tiger is officially coming out of the bag.

I like the writings of Jim Kouri. He is reasoned, articulate, and has an amazing array of sources. In a recent column, he demonstrated that people on both the Left and the Right are trying to stop Senator Hillary Clinton from becoming president. The amazing part was that even some on the Left think that she is power-mad, and that her presidency would become totalitarian. His column was very aptly titled, "Stopping Hillary Clinton is all the rage." (She tends to inspire rage in many people.)

The bottom line, from any angle you wish, is that Hillary Clinton must be stopped. I have dubbed her quest for the Oval Office as **"The Long March"**. (For those that have neglected Sun Tzu's advice to "know your enemy," the Long March was the key event that solidified the power of the Chinese Communist Party, and specifically the power of Chairman Mao Tse-Tung. If there is any doubt in your mind that Hillary Clinton is a solid Communist, then you simply haven't read enough of her own words.) She has been positioning herself to run for president for many years — certainly before her 2000 senate campaign, and probably before she became First Lady. And, for those that think Bill Clinton was a dangerous Communist (he was!), I give you this analogy. If Bill Clinton was a bear in the woods, then Hillary Clinton is a mother bear running straight at you!

why Nashville?

Coming soon, on **Tue, 23 May 2006**, the "official" presidential campaign fundraising drive of Hillary Clinton will begin. The part that amazes me is that it will begin in Nashville, Tennessee. The official statement from a campaign strategist is that it will prove that Democrats can still get strong voter support in the South. (The fact that she feels the need to prove that speaks volumes about the progress of the conservative message in recent years.) But, could there be a hidden message? With Hillary, there is *always* a hidden message. The question is: can we decipher it?

Here is an educated guess. I say educated because I organized the very first anti-Hillary campaign rally in NY State — a month before her stealth "listening tour" even began. That "tour" was then unveiled, months later, as a campaign for the US Senate. (You can read some of the details in "Staple down the tablecloths!") http://www.mensnewsdaily.com/archive/k/kovach/2004/kovach010604.htm

(More details are available in "Short Bursts: Volume 05-01") http://www.mensnewsdaily.com/archive/k/kovach/2005/kovach072805.htm

(Note: for the detail-minded, there is a slight glitch in "Staple down the tablecloths." The column was written in late December, 2003. But, it was not published until early January, 2004. Thus, it erroneously refers to "next year's presidential elections." I had no control over the publishing date.)

Nashville is the political home of Al Gore (he grew up in Carthage, but owns a home in the wealthy Belle Meade area of Nashville). It is also the home of the Music Row Democrats — famous people that don't list their names on their group's Web site. (Hmmmm. I wonder why. Can you say, "Boycott the Dixie Chicks"?) On the surface, country music has long been the realm of conservatives. But, for those of us that live in the area, we can see that many Leftists ride on the backs of those conservative singers. So, there is a lot of money available to Hillary as a result, and she is coming to Music City to collect it.

To describe the mind of Hillary Clinton, I like to use a quote from a high-ranking KGB source, who described his former boss, Mikhail Gorbachev, thusly, "He has a nice smile, but teeth of iron." Al Gore is caught in her trap. If the fundraiser succeeds, then Hillary can proudly proclaim, "You see, I don't need Al Gore." If the fundraiser fails, then Hillary can fume, "You see, Al Gore has alienated the Democrats in his own home town." Either way, Gore is brushed aside early in the "official" campaign.

My guess is that Hillary will bring along her old ally from Little Rock: General Wesley Clark. Why? Because there is a strong military presence in and around Nashville. Fort Campbell, a key resource in the War Against Terrorism, is an hour's drive from downtown. As the state capital, Nashville is home to many Guard and Reserve units. And, it is an intensely patriotic city. (During my own military career, I met more people from the Nashville area than from any other single area in the country. That was one reason why I moved here in 2001, after Hillary got elected in New York.) If he comes, Clark's presence will be to pull the patriotic Southern Democrats right into Hillary's web. (Of course, anyone associated with the Clintonistas in any way is suspect. To learn more about Clark's hidden Leftist side, read: "Wesley Clark: Discharge Immediately!")
http://www.mensnewsdaily.com/archive/k/kovach/2004/kovach020704.htm

blowback

I've used Hillary's double-edged strategies to describe the potential "blowback" to my own opponent, Congressman Jim Cooper. If he stands with Hillary at her fundraiser, then he proves that he is too far to the Left to be elected again. (Especially after he voted against HR-4437, the Border Security bill.) If he doesn't stand with her, then he proves that he is disloyal to the Leftists that are attracted to Hillary. Either way, if she comes to Nashville, she will almost certainly push the Reagan Democrat votes to me. (Thanks!)

So far, the local news media has ignored my News Release about my plans to conduct an anti-Hillary demonstration. That shouldn't surprise anyone that has followed my campaign. I filed my FEC papers on the 23rd of January, and have sent out seven campaign News Releases so far. But, there has not been one mention of my campaign in the local news media. (They also did not publicize my planned boycott of Walgreen's for supporting the "Gay" Games. But, they sure did publicize the illegal aliens' planned boycott of American businesses!) http://www.renewamerica.us/columns/kovach/060222

So, it won't surprise me if the news media makes no mention of my plans for an anti-Hillary rally on the 23rd of May. That is why this column is so necessary. (The Internet is a great leveler. That's why the UN wants to control it, and why they want to put Communist China in charge of the effort.) Please send this column to all your friends, and encourage them to join my anti-Hillary rally. http://tk-05-tn.net/Pages/Frames/stop-hillary.html

Here is the plan. **Wear blue denim overalls!** I'm serious. They are cheap, and almost everyone in middle Tennessee owns at least one set. That will show a uniform appearance. Wear a **bright colored T-shirt** — ideally, a white one with an **American flag** showing. (Sure, you can bring a small flag to wave by hand.) **If you are a military veteran, wear your uniform hat.** (There is no rule prohibiting that.) Wear boots. (Yes, I know that it might be warm that day. If you must, wear short-leg overalls. But, farmers endure discomfort all summer long, so that you and I can eat.) **Boots make noise.** If you are a military NCO veteran, and if you plan to attend the rally, then please contact me via the Web site mail form. (I want to employ your **marching experience** to help those without it.) http://tk-05-tn.net/Pages/Frames/camp-mail.html

I have contacted the Nashville mayor's office to request a parade permit. *(Did the illegal aliens have permits anywhere in the country? If so, how did they get them?)* There are two parks in close proximity to the fundraising location. My plan is to march between the two parks, thus surrounding the fundraiser with anti-Hillary chants. In May of 1999, with only two hundred people, we filled downtown Binghamton, NY, with echoing chants of, **"Go home! Go home!"** An alternative chant for Music City will be a bit more lyrical: **"Hillary... no more! Just like... Al Gore!"**

Whether we have a permit or not, we will rally near "the bells" at the north end of Bicentennial Park. Parking should be available at lunchtime on a Tuesday. (It would be even more plentiful if the State of Tennessee would give legal citizens the day off, as California did for state workers — supporting illegal aliens on Communist May Day.) We will march along Jefferson Street, and then cross it going north. We will march toward Morgan Park, and circle back. The fundraiser is located in between. (It is planned for a place called "Enchanted Gingerbread." Sounds like a place that would invite a witch.) We will continue that short circuit during the length of Hillary's stay in the neighborhood. The neighborhood is compact, and has mixed use. (There are industrial buildings, and historic homes.) The terrain is slightly sloped toward downtown. Thus, if we have a few hundred rally participants, the chants should be heard by all the Democrats inside the State Capitol, which is only a few blocks away.

By the way, I hate to bring this up, but it will cost money to buy advertising for this rally. (Given the media's track record, the only way that I'll get the word out to the local area is to pay for it myself.) Considering that being anti-Communist, anti-illegal-alien, and anti-abortion are all planks of my campaign platform, a rally against Hillary Clinton is also a rally in favor of Kovach for Congress. So, contributions to my campaign may be used to promote both my campaign and the anti-Hillary rally. (If it turns out that some minor technical rule prohibits such financial activity, then I'll simply start a separate group with a separate Web site. Right now, though, I don't think that is necessary.) Even a contribution as small as five dollars, when teamed with many other such contributions, can go a long way toward electing Tom Kovach and stopping Hillary Clinton. http://tk-05-tn.net/Pages/Frames/contribute.html

And, a vote for Tom Kovach is a vote for being vigilant in Congress, in case there should ever be a need to impeach another President Clinton.

As far as her side is concerned, the fight is on. (It has been for years.) The question is, will our side feel the same way? If you think so, then join the team! (If you are planning to come from a long distance for this rally, please contact me. The person that comes the farthest will get to address the crowd with me.) **See you at Bicentennial Park!**

NOTE: For two weeks prior to the event, the local news media did not publish any of my News Releases about it. On the morning of the event, after much prodding, the local *Tennessean* daily newspaper did print a notice in its "Datebook" section.

And, to their credit, the *Tennessean* did give news coverage of our protest activities. Of the four TV stations in Nashville, only one (WSMV, Channel 4) covered the protest. One station (WZTV Fox-17) had a crew at the fundraiser, and pointed a camera at me, but did not interview me, and did not air any footage (nor even a mention) of me.

Traffic to my campaign Web site "spiked" after coverage of the anti-Hillary event. Being against Hillary is a popular theme.

Part 5

Short Bursts

NOTE: Within the overall scope of my columns, "Short Bursts" has become my signature series. There are quite a few of them. As an example, this section contains the very first one and the latest one at the time that this collection was put together.

Short Bursts: Volume 04-01

February 9, 2004

published by: MensNewsDaily.com

Back when I used to occasionally carry an M-60 machinegun "on the job", we were taught that the most effective way to use it was in short bursts. Thus the title of this article, which debuts an occasional theme that I plan to use.

About our flag and Kid Rock

Amazingly, I have only received one piece of hate mail (so far) about that article. It is obvious that the sender must idolize Kid Rock, and therefore disbelieves anything negative that I (or anyone) might say about that boob. Thus, I am not including this information merely as a reply to that reader. Rather, this is instructive to other readers as to the caliber of people that are actually out there in the general public. The scary part is that his one vote counts the same as anyone else's in America.

Here is what that reader wrote to me:

You are a liar. You spin the news to fit your own ajenda and then blame everyone else for doing wrong. Shame on you, Jesus would be ashamed of your behavior.

Joshua — Minneapolis, MN

First of all, as my regular readers have already figured out, I abhor lying. Most of the reason that I write these columns (for free!) is to expose the truth against a background of lies and spin promulgated in the Left-leaning "mainstream" media. Secondly, there was another writer in the room that reported the same thing. Not only do I not know that other writer; but, I had tried to get a freelance assignment from the *Washington Times* for the Cash event. My recollection is that Mr. Cerveny beat me by one day. Thus, it is quite unlikely that we could've have formed a "right-wing conspiracy" about this matter. Notably, he thought Kid Rock's moronic question was important enough to put in the very first paragraph, and to allude to in the title. Clearly, I did not "spin" anything.

Secondly, for the record, "agenda" is spelled with a "g". Thirdly, I did not blame "everyone else"; I only blamed Kid Rock. He alone ripped and profaned the American flag onstage at the Super Bowl, and he deserves any consequences of his actions. (Those who enabled his wrongful acts deserve to share in those consequences.) Grammatically, "Shame on you" should have been one sentence, ended with a period. Theologically, Jesus spent the majority of His public ministry exposing the truth behind the wrongful acts of public figures; so, I doubt that He would be ashamed of my emulation of His praiseworthy example. I'm quite secure in that position, which is ultimately between Him and me.

About my analysis of Wesley Clark

As I write this, that article only appeared this morning. But, lest I be misunderstood, I have nothing against Wesley Clark the man. In fact, he has many personal qualities that I admire. (For example, he seems to demand a lot of himself, and works to ensure that he gets it.) Many of the deeds in his record are also very admirable, such as when he rappelled down a cliff to examine the wreckage of the vehicle that was blasted off that cliff during an attack on an ambassador. (I would've done the same thing in those circumstances.) He is obviously very intelligent, and quite articulate. He will do well in almost any endeavor that he chooses to undertake. But, he should not become the next president, nor should he even survive as a candidate. If he remains in the race until the convention process is over, he will likely become the next meal ticket for Bill and Hillary Clinton. That is a disaster that this country cannot afford. Unfortunately, despite all of his good qualities, General Clark has made his bed with a couple of power-hungry, not-so-closet Communists. There is a Russian proverb that my grandmother quoted often. "How you make your bed is how you'll sleep." General Clark made his bed with the Clintons and other Socialists, and it should become his political deathbed.

By the way, since the submission of yesterday's article, I've noticed a new television ad for the Clark campaign. <u>The ad contradicts itself</u>. Images of boy Clark are displayed, showing that his mother worked as a low-paid bank clerk to support him when he was growing up. He uses those images to support another hike in the minimum wage, to seven dollars per hour. (By contrast, when a young Theodore Roosevelt was working 14 to 16 hours per day as a cowboy on the open range, the pay was <u>one dollar per day</u>. So, candidate Clark thinks that scanning groceries in an air-conditioned store should be paid at a rate **168 times** that of a historic, hard-working American cowboy. This shows that Leftists have no idea that it is <u>their own policies</u> that have created much of the inflation that causes low-income people to be unable to afford things in the first place.) Every government-ordered hike in the minimum wage has resulted in overall job loss for Americans. (Remember the 1972 election? Richard Nixon, trying to buy votes by imitating the Democrats, tinkered with wages and prices. He almost lost his re-election campaign, because the public blamed him for "runaway" inflation. At that time, inflation rose to a "whopping" <u>three</u> percent! Reporters said the economy was "out of control".) This trend stretches back for decades. Ultimately, the Leftists in our government have priced non-union workers out of the market with their hikes in the minimum wage. Simultaneously, union workers have been priced out of many industries by their own leadership's constant demands for more and more, when that industry itself is facing stiff foreign competition. Ask any American steel worker ... if you can find one.

In the same campaign ad, however, General Clark proposes removing tax cuts from any company that sends jobs overseas. **<u>That is a "red herring".</u>** First of all, the left-leaning Democrats are always talking about removing tax cuts from "the rich", anyway. Considering that anyone that owns a company big enough to have enough jobs to send some of them overseas is automatically a member of "the rich", the proposal is somewhat redundant. But, it also says that Clark plans to wield the tax laws as a sword against some companies, but not others. That sounds an awful lot like Bill Clinton, who used the IRS as his personal attack dogs, setting them upon churches that preached against his anti-American, pro-homosexual, pro-Communist policies. Secondly, unless our country's elected representatives have totally lost their collective minds, such a proposal as Clark's should not be able to pass Congress, because of the potential of its aforementioned selective-targeting dangers. Clark, with his advisors in the Clinton camp, is politically savvy enough *to know that the proposal can't pass Congress.* (And, if it does, then Wesley Clark would have enormous control over what Thomas Jefferson called "the power to destroy".) So, the entire proposal is designed to "look good" to surface voters, while in reality being a totally empty cartridge on his political gunbelt. That is a quintessential "red herring", and Clark is not stupid enough to have used it unknowingly. (If he was not such a well-known intellectual, perhaps he could've *said* he didn't know.)

So, my predictions about Wesley Clark being contradictory and a Clinton clone have been proven quite correct. What did surprise me was how quickly he proved it.

After finishing this article (at least, so I thought), some reactions to my previous article about Clark have come in. One says that I quoted Col. David Hackworth's negative articles about Clark, but failed to quote the positive article. Please read my article again, sir. I gave the title of the positive article, and provided a link to it, with a notation that I wanted to be balanced. But, I also noted that Hackworth's negative articles about Clark outnumber it three-to-one.

Another reader, "R" from Houston, had this to say.

I don't believe you will thank me for contacting you. Hmm, you have betrayed American values and lied through your teeth for right wing idealogues who are betraying my country. If you don't like it, then leave. I believe that is what you and your ilk are always telling us.

Again, I truly despise lying. I researched sources from the Right, from the Left, from the extreme Left, and from Clark's own campaign Web site. (That would supposedly be the "middle", correct? And, you would consider me the "extreme" Right, correct?) This may surprise you, "R", but I actually admire what little I know about the man Wesley Clark. I'm sure that, in a personal meeting, we could both be congenial. And, in a firefight, we'd both be sending bullets in the same direction. But, the facts are the facts. And, the fact is that he would be a bad choice for president.

By the way, I'm not quite sure how using my First Amendment right to free speech, in a responsible manner, with plenty of supporting facts, is an example of "betraying American values". After all, wasn't warning the American public *exactly* what Benjamin Franklin and Alexander Hamilton did with their publishing? Wasn't that what Samuel Adams did with the town meetings at his pub? And, wasn't that what Paul Revere did with his famous midnight ride? How, "R", did I betray American values? Wanting to have a president that upholds the Constitution and its principles, as articulated by those that wrote it, is what I'm after. (And, don't think I don't notice the problems with our current occupant of the White House. Right now, I'm focusing on Clark because the primary is coming up in the state where I live.) If you can explain how using supported facts to tell the truth is a betrayal of American values, then please feel free to send me your explanation. (By the way, considering that Clark is *not yet even in power*, why would "R" tell me to leave? If that is an example of the mindset of Clark's followers, then it's a good thing that I wrote that article. What will happen if Clark is elected? Will people like "R" become deputized to round up people like me?)

About our military in general.

It's no surprise to regular readers that I have enormous respect (dare I say "love"?) for the institution of our military and for its people (with a few, rare exceptions). So, it is with joy that I pass along this link to you. I got it in an e-mail from my father-in-law, who is a retired Army intelligence major. It is a slide show of the "year in pictures" for the Army in 2003. If you don't get choked up seeing some of these photos, then contact your psychiatrist immediately.

Respect for our American flag

The item above, coupled with my article about Kid Rock, should leave no doubt about how I feel about respect for our flag. But, words often pale in comparison to certain pictures. (Thanks, again, to my father-in-law for sending this link along.) No opinion that I could write could compare to the pictures and facts about <u>this one military funeral</u>. God bless that young man's soul, his family, and that Texas town. Somehow, I doubt that Kid Rock would be welcome there.

Now, it's time to let my barrel cool off for awhile. "Reloading!"

Short Bursts: Volume 06-03

Aid & comfort, United 93, political hurdles

April 25, 2006

Despite the fact that bad things happen in our world, and despite the fact that the "mainstream" media (MSM) continues to ignore both my columns and my campaign, some things just keep on improving. For example, my columns have now been picked up by yet another publication: Sierra Times. That introduces a whole new reader segment to the world of Tom Kovach, and to this occasional series of Short Bursts.

aid and comfort

The Constitution of the United States includes in the definition of treason (Article III, Section 3): "adhering to their Enemies, giving them Aid and Comfort." Despite the dedicated work of many Leftists within our government, America remains "that shining city upon a hill." I'm worried that we don't shine as brightly as we did in decades past. I'm worried that the hill has become charred and pockmarked from the constant shelling from the Left. But, overall, America is still America.

That is why it galls me that the President of the United States has recently come out and said that rounding up and deporting illegal aliens is "not going to work". Oh, really? There is a Chinese proverb that says, "The man who says that a task is impossible should get out of the way of the man doing it." If our president feels that America is incapable of expelling illegal aliens, then he should just get all of the Federal agents out of the way, and let the volunteer Minuteman Project do the job that our agents are *prevented* from doing. Private citizens have already volunteered to watch our borders, and to build the fences that the government neglects. I'm sure that more volunteers would gladly help to protect our homes and jobs, by rounding up the illegals, given that our president thinks it isn't worth even trying.

There is a fatal flaw in President Bush's presentation: America has enemies. Some of those enemies are intent upon entering our country, with the goal of destroying us. Not all of America's enemies plan to sneak in quietly. Some of our enemies talk of massive invasion. China's military is almost as large as our entire population. North Korea's army is the largest, per capita, in the world. Recently, there has been much anti-American rhetoric from the president of Venezuela. Some analysts think that the next president of Mexico could attempt the *Reconquista* option. (If our own president doesn't do it for them.) And, don't forget that Cuba is still run by Castro's Communists.

Given that so many foreign countries seem to at least consider invading America as a possible option, and given that some of those countries have armies larger than the number of illegal aliens within the United States, does it seem foolish to anyone else that the President of the United States would say that getting rid of foreign invaders (they are *not* "guests"!) is not going to work? Perhaps our president thinks that rounding up illegal aliens is one of those "jobs that Americans won't do." Perhaps some might say that such a statement meets the definition of giving "aid and comfort" to our enemies.

United 93

This coming Friday (28 Apr 2006), the movie "United 93" is scheduled to premiere for general audiences. It has already been screened by some reporters, and opens today at the Tribecca Film Festival. Televised previews promise a gritty, realistic presentation. That also seems to be the sentiment of most reviews. But, just *how realistic* can the movie actually be?

I continue to stand firm by my five-part presentation that Flight 93 was shot down. Regular readers will recall that I published that series to refute comments made during a Discovery Channel documentary, "Flight 93: the flight that fought back". While there are some that will parrot charges of "conspiracy theory," I can stand proud upon the message that I got from the father of one of Flight 93's ill-fated passengers. He said that someone was finally telling the truth. (He had withheld that comment from other presenters of shoot-down scenarios, because they speculated rather than examined the evidence.) I've received similar comments from the father of a Flight 800 victim.

Quite telling is the fact that the producers admit that the movie was originally called "Flight 93," *but the title was changed* to "United 93." There are more than 6.5-million Web pages that come up in a Google search of the term "Flight 93." The *very first one* (based on relevance; i.e.: number of page views) is a collection of evidence that supports the shoot-down scenario. So, if the title of the movie had remained "Flight 93," and if people had looked up the movie title on Google, they would've *first* found several references to the shoot-down scenario. Apparently, the movie's producers didn't want that to happen. If one goes to Google, and looks up "United 93," the first several pages of responses have to do only with the movie. (Interestingly, if one Googles the two phrases "Flight 93" and "shot down," there are 126,000 replies. My column is number 13 out of all those replies. And, as the movie renews interest in the topic, that ranking might improve even further.)

One of the key supports of the shoot-down scenario is the seismic evidence. The cockpit voice recorder (CVR) tape stops at 1003 on that fateful day. But, a seismograph in western Pennsylvania records the crash at 1006. Naysayers try to claim that the information is faulty, because a scientist that gained fame by writing a report about the seismic evidence has recently recanted his position. (Was he threatened with the cutoff of government research contract money?) However, there are *other* scientists that still stand by the position that: A) there is a three-minute gap between the end of the CVR tape and the seismic recording of the plane's impact; and, B) seconds before the plane's impact, the seismograph recorded an "N-curve" that indicates a sonic boom. Given that the airliner was not capable of supersonic speed, there had to be another source for the sonic boom. The logical source is a pursuing fighter jet.

The producers of "United 93" have promised to donate 10% of the profits to support a memorial for the victims. But, the design of the Flight 93 memorial honors the terrorists. (Some people disagree, but I don't see how. The memorial is shaped like the Star-and-Crescent shape of the emblem of Islam. The only Muslims aboard that flight were the hijackers. Should we spend tax money on *that*?) I have not been privy to an advance screening of "United 93"; but, the early signals are that they will try to pooh-pooh the shoot-down scenario. Considering that the Federal government came up with several different versions of the timeline of the scrambling of fighter jets, it seems obvious that they're covering up something. The debris field is consistent with a shoot-down (*not* by a missile, but by cannon fire). Given the likelihood that "United 93" will ignore evidence of a shoot-down, I don't see how it can be a "realistic" movie. Thus, I don't plan to support it with my money.

political hurdles

If elected to Congress, I might obtain access to government records about Flight 93, Flight 800, and other controversies. And, if evidence of the downings of those airliners were revealed, then the MSM would have a lot of explaining to do. Perhaps that explains why the MSM has ignored my campaign for Congress.

Unfortunately, the liberals are not the only ones that have ignored my campaign. Conservative voters might be surprised to discover how many "conservative" political organizations have ignored it, also. I'm reminded of the famous quote by Thomas

Jefferson: "The making of laws, like the making of sausage, is not for the squeamish to watch."

Just yesterday, I was on the phone with the director one such organization. They are a single-issue political action committee (PAC). The issue is one that conservatives take very seriously: abortion. Back in February, I had gone to their Web site, requested an endorsement, and sent in a completed candidate questionnaire. No one responded. I sent follow-up e-mails. No one responded. I finally made a phone call. The director called me back. I asked if she had visited my Web site. She replied "no." She said that she had received the first page of my faxed questionnaire back in February. (Nobody ever contacted me to say that the fax was not complete.) The *very first question* was, "How much money have you raised?"

I have not raised much money at all. How can I? Few people know about my campaign. How can they know, when I haven't advertised? How can I advertise, when I don't have much money? How can I raise money, when few people know about my campaign? Isn't that what PACs are for? But, if the PACs won't give you money until you've *already* raised money, then the only people that can get elected are people that are *already* wealthy. And, don't many voters agree that *wealthy people* in office have agendas that go against the average voter? Yet, it seems that the voters don't have a choice.

The Internet is "a great leveler." In theory, a candidate with almost no money can challenge a wealthy incumbent on a level playing field. I'm not good at raising money. And, I'm not good at begging. I know how hard it is for the Average Joe to get by, because it's that hard for me, too. So, I'm really reluctant to ask other people to give money — even though my campaign can't compete without it. (Even a business-card-size ad in the newspaper, with nothing but my Web site address, costs $400 per day. The site only costs me $10 per month; but, I have to get people *to the site*.)

I've made it as easy as possible for people to donate to my campaign. But, so far, *only three people* have done so in the four months since my initial FEC filing. Because I write my own speeches, my own ad copy, my own HTML code for the Web site, etc., I don't need to pay consultants. (I've even developed a way for *other people* to print my campaign signs — almost *for free*.) But, because of the "dumbing down" of our classrooms, and the "expert mentality" (someone else knows better than you), and the "welfare mentality" (if it's important, the government will pay to do it for you), our society doesn't seem to realize that it takes *all of us* to stop the Leftists from destroying what's left of America. People seem to assume that anyone running for Congress already has a silver spoon in their mouth. I certainly don't.

During the summer when I investigated this vehicle bombing (for free), I also worked on a horse ranch and an asphalt crew. (Hey, President Bush, did you know that a guy with a paralegal certificate was shoveling horse poop? So, name a job that Americans won't do, OK?) I know that five dollars can be the difference between eating and not eating after a hard day's work. But, I also know that five dollars could be the difference between stopping the Socialists in our government and not stopping them. (I'd rather have a thousand contributions of $20 than twenty contributions of $1,000, because those big contributions sometimes come with a lot of strings attached.) If only a thousand people (out of more than 100,000 voters) in my district would give only five dollars a month (*regularity* is the key), then I could win the election. Some people could afford $100 per month. With that, I could buy TV ads (necessary in our illiterate society) that would make the issues plain for anyone to understand. And, it's OK for people outside my district to contribute, also. (Out of the three contributors so far, one of them is a former Blue Beret from another state.)

My campaign treasurer (my wife) got irritated over one of my fundraising ideas. Having jumped out of helicopters a few dozen times during my military career, I know how much beer is consumed in the military. My concept was to ask those troops that agree with my campaign to "sacrifice" the cost of just one pitcher of beer to support it. The concept was called "Pitchers for Politics". It was just a catchy way to ask the "little guy" to get on board a big idea. But, my wife talked me out of that one. So, if you are in the military, or if you know someone in the military, or if you know someone that drinks beer, then you don't have to send them the above link — because that fundraising concept was never officially implemented (it has no Web page); therefore, it doesn't officially exist. But, if it did exist, it would probably become quite successful, because most of our troops are quite conservative.

Well, for the moment, I'm pinned down in a media quagmire. But, I'm confident that resupply and reinforcements are on the way. **Dig in!**

Section 6

Poetry and Lyrics

NOTE: As an avid listener to talk-radio, and to G. Gordon Liddy's show in particular, I submitted this spoof song as a tribute theme song.

Much to my surprise, Mr. Liddy first *sang* it on the air, and then later had it recorded to sound like the original.

The Ballad of the Liddy Brigade

to the melody of: "The Ballad of the Green Berets"
(original words & music by Barry Sadler,
Staff Sgt., US Army, Special Forces)

Fighting liberals, on the air.
Here's a man who has no hair.
He speaks his mind, and he'll let you...
if you call his talk-show, too.

In Watergate, he wouldn't talk.
His silence made the Congress balk.
So, they put him in the Federal pen.
But, look out now! He's out again!

Yes, Gordon Liddy's on the air.
Call his talk-show, if you dare!
The liberals think they've got it made.
But, they can't stop the Liddy Brigade!

(Slowly, with feeling)

This year, some kids will graduate
whom liberals tried to indoctrinate.
But, their education starts today;
'cause they just joined the Liddy Brigade.

(Upbeat, with pride)

Silver headphones on their ears.
Their presence causing liberals fears.
They worry that we'll vote someday.
Come on, join up! The Liddy Briga-a-ade....

NOTE: This next set of lyrics was written for a specific country singer, after an incident in which an elderly couple was beaten and robbed at an upscale shopping mall in Nashville. I kept thinking that the husband should've been armed.

Standoff

© 2002

A couple walked back to their car
        from an evening on the town.
It had been a long time since
        she'd worn an evening gown.

She was looking elegant,
        and he was feeling proud.
And neither was expecting
        the shouts that came so loud.

"Get down on the ground right now!
        And give me all your cash!
And if you don't I'm gonna give
        your wife a bloody gash!"

They both looked at each other
        and knew what they should do.
And their story is a lesson now
        that I'll impart to you.

The wife was crying loudly
        as her man pulled out his cash.
The robber kept his eye on him,
        and told him to move fast.

Then the robber told the wife
        to open up her purse.
She did as she was told, you know,
        and the robber's day got worse.

She pulled out the gun that
        her man had given her.
And shot that robber twice, so fast
        that his eyes began to blur.

The woman told her husband,
        "I knew that you were right."
The lessons that you gave me then
        protected us tonight.

The couple went back home that night,
        and thanked God they were alive.
The next day they told all their friends
        about how they did survive.

And now I'm here to tell you, friend,
        take heed while you still can.
That is why the right to arms
        is for each American.

So steel your mind for self-defense,
        then put steel in your hand.
And don't let fear invade your mind,
        or steal freedom from our land.

NOTE: Most of us remember that the "9-11" attacks happened on a Tuesday morning. By Wednesday afternoon, I had begun to form the concept for a song. That evening, the most important aspect of the song became part of a prayer that I offered aloud in a special church service. That following Saturday morning, I sat down at a computer and typed out the lyrics of this song.

Considering that I live in the Nashville area, one might think that it would be easy for even a non-musical person (such as me) to get a song idea out of one's head, onto paper, and then sung and recorded by talented people. Ha! The streets of downtown are littered with sad people that took all their money to come here for that very purpose. And, most of those homeless people can sing! So, by contrast, a guy like me has a hard row to hoe. (My singing voice was once described as "similar to the sound of two chalkboards mating".)

Even though I go to church with many people that write and/or sing songs for a living, no one at church was any help. All they did was tell me how difficult (or "impossible") my project would be.

But, by the grace of God, I met a musical "transcriptionist", who makes his living by pulling songs out of people's heads and putting the songs onto paper. (I met him by trying to sell him a car!) In only two hours, he did for me what three years of asking "friends" at church could not produce. He didn't charge much; and, he lived walking distance from my house. (In fact, years prior, I had my first in-person encounter with Johnny Cash right near the house where the transcriptionist lived. Small world.)

This song has a slow, ballad melody.

One Day

© 2001

Thousands of people went to work one day –
    with no idea what would come their way.
They just went out to pursue their dreams –
    American dreams – of what could be … one day….

A small group of people went to work one day.
> The things they did would hold the world at bay.

The shock, the horror, and the pure dismay
> at what those terrorists did one day.

Around the world, more people heard the news that day.
> And they wondered how things ever got this way.

They hoped that something like that wouldn't
> befall them ... one day.

America stood paralyzed, for just one day.
> And then the sleeping giant vowed to make them pay.

They can run, but they will not outrun that day.
> Our country will put a stop to them ... one day.

The attack was meant to drive us to our knees that day.
> It did, but that was when America began to pray.

We joined the families with the hope that they
> Will see their loved ones once again ... one day.
>> ... one day
>>> ... one day.

MORE NOTES: Several people in the music business have told me that this song would sound better from a woman's voice than a man's. I have a friend at church with a great voice. She loves to sing. But, making a recording costs money — unless, of course, one has a wealthy investor to provide some backing.

This woman has survived **four brain tumors in one spot!** She deserves a break. So, if you are a wealthy investor, and would like to help this woman have an income from music, please contact me. I've made enough contacts in Nashville to be able to set up a recording, once the money is available. (Actually, somebody should make a documentary about her life. She is too modest. But, if she could make money singing, then I know she would enjoy that tremendously.)

NOTE: This last one is a cowboy poem. A couple of years ago, a high-paying office job was mighty hard to find. (After "9-11", many people withdrew lawsuits. Thus, paralegal work was hard to find.) So, I worked at a trail-riding ranch. My job title was "wrangler". I got paid to help care for a herd of 24 horses, and to lead trail rides, and to give riding lessons. Some days, I was in the saddle almost all day. The job was physically demanding, but so much fun. I rode my first horse in Texas at age six, rode an unbroken colt at age 12, and owned two horses (with my first wife) when I was in the Air Force. I love horses, and this poem reflects the fact that I was privileged to be able to drive outside of Nashville every day and live out an *old-fashioned* life. (Then, go home and type up this poem on the *computer*!)

Why I wrangle

© 2004

Some people actually ask why
    I do a job where I might die
        from gettin' kicked or dragged.
They just don't seem to understand
    this kind of work, or this kind of man —
        who'd die from gettin' nagged.

It might surprise a few to learn
    that there's more to life than cash to earn,
        and more to a life's work than just the *work*.

And it also might surprise them
    to read my "ray-zew-may",
        and learn that I've done many jobs
            that earned a *lot* more pay.

But those jobs were all just ... jobs —
    while wranglin' is a life.
It really is a calling —
    it's almost like a wife.

The office politics out here
    takes place in the corral,
Where snorts, and bites, and kicks, and charges
    replace the rumor mill.

The whirring of the copier,
    and the pounding of the keys,
        has been replaced by hoofbeats
            and the wind among the trees.

I didn't have to fill out
    any fancy application form.
All I did was demonstrate
    that *honor* is my norm.

We all care for the horses that God put here to ride.
    Their lives depend on us, and we take the pain in stride —
        because the thunder of their hooves
            can fill our hearts with pride.

So, when some slicker asks me,
    "You do *what* kind of work?!"
I just let the question dangle,
    because some folks could never understand
        why I chose to wrangle.

Index

nicknames & phrases

"Cotton-Eyed Joe" 89	**"The Long March"** 162
"dragon burp" 76	"ethnic cleansing" 107
"Electronic slide" 94	"Mainstream" Media [MSM]
"guest legislator" 85, 86, 87	 31
"Texas side-step." 89	"Mister Ponytail" 158

"professional hit" 119

A

Afghanistan 21, 22, 74, 76, 145, 148
Air Force 3, 6, 8, 23, 25, 27, 34, 35, 40, 73, 83, 100, 104
Air National Guard . 39, 40, 42, 43, 44
Airborne 21, 22
al-Qaida 28, 112, 133
American cowboy 174
anti-abortion 33, 54, 168
anti-Hillary rally 166, 168
anti-terrorism 73
Arab 111, 112, 114
Armed Services Committee 146
Army . 1, 14, 15, 17, 18, 33, 42, 43, 55, 75, 76, 78, 83, 102, 113, 133, 178
ATF 117, 118, 122, 123, 128

B

Baader-Meinhof Gang 113
Balkans 91, 107, 141
battle 21, 29, 35
Belgium 102, 103, 105
Bethlehem 102
Black and conservative 48
Blackhawk 8
bombing 104, 113, 117, 121, 123, 124, 125, 126, 128, 140, 186
Bonnie and Clyde 115
Border Patrol 57, 95
Border Security 46, 165
borders .. 51, 52, 53, 56, 57, 67, 68, 73, 75, 77, 78, 79, 80, 85, 88, 90, 91, 92, 94, 95, 96, 97, 98, 180
briefcase 17, 18, 19, 20, 28, 145
Brown Berets 47, 49, 50, 53, 54, 56, 58
Bubba Doublewide 153
Bush 7, 17, 149

C

C-130 .... 21, 25, 27
California1, 50, 57, 70, 82, 167
Capitol 83, 86, 87, 168
Casey Sheehan 31, 33, 37
Catholic 32, 107, 142
Cecil Rhodes 138, 142
Center for Immigration Studies 80
Cheney 17, 20, 145
child molester 33
Chinese proverb 24, 180
Christian ... 26, 33, 49, 84, 107, 108, 132, 141, 142
Christianity 26, 108
Christopher Chandler 21
CIA 6, 8, 18
Cindy Sheehan .. 29, 30, 31, 32, 33, 37
citizens .. 19, 47, 53, 65, 67, 68, 69, 78, 80, 93, 96, 97, 103, 108, 111, 136, 148, 156, 158, 167, 180
Civil Air Patrol 40
classified 100, 104, 113
Clinton 8, 56, 107, 134, 138, 139, 141, 142, 144, 146, 152, 153, 154, 158, 159, 160, 161, 162, 164, 168, 169, 173, 175
Col. Charlie Beckwith 26

combat.................3, 18, 33, 154
commander..14, 16, 18, 40, 44, 78
Commander-in-Chief...36, 146
Commie-speak ..155, 156, 157, 159
Communism.52, 54, 55, 56, 69
Communist China........91, 166
Communist Party ..52, 87, 155, 162
Communists ..3, 52, 53, 56, 69, 109, 153, 154, 155, 157, 158, 159, 173, 181
Congress. B, 12, 73, 82, 84, 89, 90, 91, 97, 154, 155, 168, 169, 175, 184, 186
congressional..................33, 98
Congressional hearing..........83
conservatives...37, 54, 67, 164, 184
Constitution.48, 57, 77, 88, 90, 177, 179
Constitutional.....49, 57, 58, 98
counter-terrorism..................73
crash.........39, 60, 73, 132, 183

D
Deaf.......................................79
declassified...........55, 104, 114
Delta Force.........................25
Democrat......33, 142, 145, 165
Democratic Party 57, 145, 153, 158, 161
Desert Storm 92
Director of Central Intelligence96, 150
DMZ..............................74, 92
documentation........................B
downsized 26, 73
Dr. Alan Keyes..............47, 54

E
Egyptian...............................92
explosives.....21, 103, 119, 120
explosives ordnance disposal (EOD)..............................21

F
Farsi....................................70
FBI.....................................118
Figueroa. 39, 40, 41, 42, 43, 44
firepower..................30, 76, 79
First Lady...........153, 160, 162
Flight 93.......45, 181, 182, 183, 184
Fort Benning..................21, 22
Frank Kovach 1
freedom.....19, 20, 52, 62, 111, 134
Freedom From War..........93
Full Metal Jacket.................29
fundraiser......B, 164, 165, 167, 169

G
George Washington.............49
Globalism 93
God . 27, 28, 38, 108, 109, 158, 159, 178
Guatemala...........................80
Haiti.............................91, 141
Heartland America...............84
Hebrew 70
helicopter.....27, 39, 45, 50, 76
helicopters............25, 116, 187
Hillary...31, 56, 134, 142, 144, 146, 152, 154, 155, 156, 157, 158, 159, 160, 161, 162, 163, 164, 165, 166, 167, 168, 169, 173

hostages........... 25, 27, 110, 116
HR-4437 165

I

ideology 47, 53, 109, 155
illegal aliens 72, 93, 94, 95, 166, 167, 180, 181
illegal immigrants ... 57, 64, 65, 71, 80
immigrant.............................. 1
infiltrated........................ 20, 56
Iran 25, 26, 27, 28, 96, 110
Iranian 25, 27, 116, 149
Iraq 16, 17, 18, 19, 29, 38, 111, 141, 146, 148
Iraqi 14, 17, 19, 20, 78, 141, 148
Ireland 103, 114
Islamist.. 51, 53, 104, 108, 109, 112, 113
Israeli 102

J

Jesus 26, 32, 39, 40, 44, 102, 171, 172
Jesus Figueroa 39, 40, 44
job opportunities 88
Joe Sixpack 110, 157
John Kerry 147
Judith Hope 158, 161

K

Kandahar........................ 21, 23
Kid Rock 171, 172, 178
Korea 7, 52, 62, 74, 91, 180
Korean................ 62, 70, 74, 92

L

La Raza 54

law enforcement 73, 77, 115
Lebanon 103, 157
Leftist 31, 55, 91, 111, 137, 147, 152, 157, 158, 159, 165
Leftists 80, 100, 136, 164, 165, 174, 179, 186
Left-leaning 31, 47, 48, 49, 54, 67, 82, 114, 172
Liar-In-Chief 107
Lieutenant Colonel Allen B. West...................... 14, 78
Little Rock 134, 138, 158, 161, 164
lobbyist 45, 157
Los Angeles............. 69, 70, 71
LTC West ... 14, 15, 16, 18, 79

M

machinegun 74, 171
Maguire 42, 43, 45
Marine 1, 13, 21, 22, 23, 25, 51, 104
Marine Corps........... 13, 22, 25
Marines................ 24, 103, 104
Marxist 50, 53, 54
Mattachine Society 159
Mechistas............................ 70
media bias............................ 99
MensNewsDaily.com ... 14, 17, 21, 25, 29, 36, 50, 102, 106, 110, 136, 145, 152, 171
Mexico.. 51, 56, 57, 58, 68, 70, 80, 181
Michael Jackson 33
military 1, 7, 13, 14, 15, 16, 17, 18, 21, 26, 28, 34, 35, 38, 39, 40, 41, 42, 43, 44, 48, 68, 73, 76, 77, 78, 83, 90, 92, 94, 102, 104, 120, 134,

139, 141, 145, 147, 157, 164, 166, 177, 178, 180, 187
Military Police 77
militia 48, 49, 103
Militias 77
Minuteman .. 47, 50, 53, 82, 83, 90, 91, 180
Minutemen .. 47, 53, 54, 57, 77, 82, 91
movie 29, 89, 181, 182, 184
MSM 30, 31, 38, 47, 48, 49, 50, 52, 53, 54, 55, 69, 87, 100, 179, 184
Munich 105
Music Row Democrats 137, 164

N

Nashville 8, 64, 68, 72, 106, 117, 118, 123, 125, 128, 133, 162, 163, 164, 165, 167, 169
National Guard troops 94
New York .. 1, 2, 34, 42, 47, 60, 63, 108, 145, 152, 157, 158, 161, 165
New York blizzard 47
Newburgh 44
Nicaragua 123
novels 6
NY State 42, 63, 152, 154, 158, 163

O

Oliver North 96
One Day 193
Operation Eagle Claw 27
Opryland 118, 122, 126
Osama bin-Laden 28, 112, 133, 134

P

Palestinian 102
parachute 8, 35, 83
parallel universe 66, 85
passing lane 60, 61, 63
Paul A. Weaver, Jr. 44
Pentagon 28, 36, 148
Persian Gulf 109
police 14, 15, 19, 50, 65, 66, 78, 85, 86, 87, 114, 118, 123, 125, 126, 127, 128, 132
Pravda 47
Predator 96, 97
president . 7, 19, 29, 30, 31, 37, 38, 47, 56, 90, 94, 134, 138, 139, 140, 141, 143, 148, 149, 161, 162, 173, 176, 177, 180, 181
President Andrew Jackson. 138
President Bush .. 16, 19, 29, 30, 31, 32, 37, 57, 90, 94, 95, 97, 98, 146, 147, 148, 149, 180, 186
Progressive Caucus 155

Q

R

Reagan ... 27, 73, 96, 111, 116, 149, 153, 165
RenewAmerica.us ... 39, 45, 47, 59, 65, 82, 89, 94, 161
Republican .. 33, 34, 37, 47, 55, 113, 137, 141, 145
rifle 29, 104
road rage 59, 64
ROK Rangers 75
Ron Paul 86

S

Saddam Hussein 14, 15, 17, 18, 19, 79, 138, 145, 147, 149
Schwarzenegger 57
Search and Rescue 27
security.. 49, 51, 56, 57, 68, 73, 75, 79, 93, 94, 95, 98, 103, 104, 111, 115, 116, 132
Senate 31, 84, 86, 159, 161, 163
Senator Kennedy 80
<u>Short Bursts</u> 163, 170, 171, 179
slingshot effect 9, 11, 12
sniper 29
Socialist.. 31, 57, 109, 140, 142
soldier 7, 29, 74, 75
soldiers .. 6, 15, 16, 30, 96, 107, 143, 146
Somalia 7, 49
Soviet Union 47, 74
Special Forces 75
Special Operations 6, 7, 17, 23, 91
Spectre 76, 77
SR-71 150
Standoff 191
Stewart ANG Base 44
surveillance 78, 95, 97

T

Tanzim 103
Ted Kennedy 68, 80
Tehran 25, 73, 74, 104, 110, 115, 149
Tennessee 60, 64, 80, 136, 137, 138, 163, 166, 167
Terri Schiavo 32, 33
terrorism 55, 104, 110, 111, 112, 113, 114, 117, 118, 123, 132
terrorist 26, 28, 44, 51, 76, 100, 103, 108, 110, 111, 112, 113, 114
terrorists 6, 24, 51, 53, 78, 100, 103, 106, 107, 108, 109, 112, 114, 134, 183
Texas 2, 51, 54, 57, 59, 61, 70, 89, 90, 94, 98, 178
The Ballad of the Liddy Brigade 189
Thomas P. Maguire 42, 45
Tom Tancredo 86
Tony Dolz 82
traitors 71, 79
Trojan horse 96
TWA Flight 800 39
tyrannical 20, 104, 111

U

Ukrainian 70
union 57, 72, 136, 174
United 93 .. 179, 181, 182, 183
United States 3, 28, 36, 48, 49, 53, 56, 57, 62, 65, 67, 69, 70, 71, 77, 80, 82, 92, 94, 98, 108, 134, 136, 138, 152, 154, 157, 161, 179, 180, 181
unmanned aerial vehicles (UAVs) 76
Upstate 1, 8, 63, 89
US House of Representatives 71
USAF 3, 7, 36, 77
USMC 22

V

Vice President Cheney 19

Vietnam........................3, 29, 92
vote.........70, 71, 154, 169, 171

W

Walter Reed 23, 83
War Powers...........................49
Washington Times...............172
Wesley Clark ...131, 133, 136, 137, 138, 140, 142, 143, 164, 173, 175, 176

whistleblower 35, 39
White House ... 7, 87, 147, 153, 160, 177
Why I wrangle 195
William Casey 96
WorldNetDaily 9, 14, 111

XYZ

www.ingramcontent.com/pod-product-compliance
Lightning Source LLC
Chambersburg PA
CBHW032046150426
43194CB00006B/438